TOTAL GOLF TECHNIQUES

Also by Jack Nicklaus (with Ken Bowden and Jim McQueen)

GOLF MY WAY

TOTAL GOLF TECHNIQUES

BY **JACK NICKLAUS**

WITH KEN BOWDEN

ILLUSTRATED BY JIM McQUEEN

HEINEMANN : LONDON

William Heinemann Ltd
15 Queen Street, Mayfair, London W1X 8BE

LONDON   MELBOURNE   TORONTO
JOHANNESBURG   AUCKLAND

SBN 434 51351 2

Published originally as the Jack Nicklaus
Lesson Tee series in Golf Digest Magazine, U.S.A.

Printed in Great Britain by
Jarrold & Sons Ltd, Norwich

INTRODUCTION

One of my greatest assets as a golfer has been my day-to-day ability to doctor my own swing. I've often gone back to my original teacher, Jack Grout, for checkups and review sessions but rarely for major surgery. The reason is that whenever a serious swing problem has arisen—and I've had a few in my time—I've generally been able to work it out via my own understanding of golfing cause and effect.

That ability did not happen by accident. Virtually from the time I started playing golf I have studied the "why" as well as the "how" of the game's technique. It has never been enough for me simply to hit good shots: I've always wanted to know precisely *what caused* the good shots, just as much as I've wanted to know *what caused* the bad shots. This pursuit of basic cause-and-effect knowledge has stayed with me over the years. It's one reason I've felt that I could continue to improve as a golfer so long as I was prepared to make the necessary effort.

I make this point here because I think it relates to the most important information other golfers might gain from this book.

Most golfers do not play poorly because they lack physical ability, or even because they lack practice. I know lots of athletic types who practice furiously without ever getting much better. The reason most golfers play less well than they'd like—and could—is that they basically do not understand what they should be trying to achieve with a golf club.

The finest way to obtain that knowledge, as I was fortunate enough to be able to do, is through concentrated instruction from a skilled teacher, plus regular and thoughtful practice, and intensive competition. But lack of time alone makes that impossible for most people. It is in this respect that the printed word becomes valuable. Although I've never believed it possible to become a fine golfer simply by reading about the game, I've also never doubted that it's a valid way to obtain a fundamental *understanding* of golf. Without that, lasting improvement is impossible.

This book covers a great deal of ground; in fact, it contains pretty much everything I know about the mechanics of the game. In consequence, the specifics of technique are depicted and described in great detail—albeit as directly and simply as possible. Hopefully, this detailed treatment of the various shots and swing techniques will be helpful to readers. But the principal value of the book to the majority of golfers, I hope and believe, will lie in its explanation and depiction of the *basic goals of swinging a golf club.*

In working on my own game, I try never to practice the *how* without mentally giving myself the *why*. We have tried to do the same thing here in each self-contained "lesson." Thus the general theme of *Lesson Tee* might fairly be described as the *fundamental cause and effect factors* of playing golf. If you study, practice and adhere to them, you are bound to become a better player.

I'd like to say a word about how *Lesson Tee* came into being and how it was created. On the principle that "one picture is worth a thousand words," the editors of *Golf Digest* magazine came up with the idea of a "cartoon-type" presentation in the early 1970s when Ken Bowden was editorial director of the magazine. To do the art work, I recommended Jim McQueen, who happened at that time to be the pro at a course I had designed near my home in Florida. Jim previously had been a full-time artist who had worked for *Golf Digest* and other

publications. I felt his style had clarity, simplicity and directness.

The "Lesson Tee" feature began to run in the March 1972 issue of *Golf Digest* and concluded in the March 1976 issue. The creative process over that four-year period consisted of my putting the words on tape, Ken Bowden organizing them onto paper, and finally Jim McQueen adding his marvelous drawings. All three of us owe thanks to the editors and art staff of *Golf Digest* for their creative contributions and support.

Throughout the publication of the Lesson Tee articles, I've received more kind comments about them than I have about any previous literary effort, and I understand they quickly became the best-read features in the history of *Golf Digest*.

I have always regarded my authorship efforts primarily as a chance to offer something back to the game that has been so good to me. It is my sincere hope that this book will contribute to the greater golfing enjoyment of anyone who reads it.

Jack Nicklaus

JACK NICKLAUS' CAREER RECORD

MAJOR TOURNAMENTS

Nicklaus has won 16 major tournaments through 1976, more than any other player in the history of the game.

MASTERS: 1963, 1965, 1966, 1972, 1975
U.S. OPEN: 1962, 1967, 1972
PGA: 1963, 1971, 1973, 1975
BRITISH OPEN: 1966, 1970
U.S. AMATEUR: 1959, 1961

VICTORIES, YEAR BY YEAR

Nicklaus has captured 63 tour events since starting his professional career in January, 1962, through September, 1976.

1959 U.S. Amateur
1961 U.S. Amateur
1962 U.S. Open, Seattle World's Fair, Portland
1963 Palm Springs, Masters, Tournament of Champions, PGA Championship, Sahara
1964 Portland, Tournament of Champions, Phoenix, Whitemarsh
1965 Portland, Masters, Memphis, Thunderbird Classic, Philadelphia
1966 Masters, Sahara, National Team (with Arnold Palmer), British Open
1967 U.S. Open, Sahara, Bing Crosby, Western, Westchester
1968 Western, American Golf Classic
1969 Sahara, Kaiser, San Diego
1970 Byron Nelson, British Open, Four-Ball (with Arnold Palmer)
1971 PGA Championship, Tournament of Champions, Byron Nelson, National Team (with Arnold Palmer), Disney World
1972 Bing Crosby, Doral-Eastern, Masters, U.S. Open, Westchester, Match Play, Disney
1973 Bing Crosby, New Orleans, Tournament of Champions, Atlanta, PGA Championship, Ohio Kings Island, Walt Disney
1974 Hawaii, Tournament Players Championship
1975 Doral-Eastern Open, Heritage Classic, Masters, PGA Championship, World Open
1976 Tournament Players Championship, World Series of Golf

PLAYOFF RECORD: won 8 out of 11
CAREER EARNINGS: $2,803,542 (through World Series of Golf, 1976)
MOST MONEY WON ON TOUR IN ONE YEAR (1972): $320,542
OTHER ACHIEVEMENTS:
PGA Player-of-the-Year, 1967, 1972, 1973, 1975
Ryder Cup Team, 1969, 1971, 1973, 1975
Member of the winning U.S. World Cup Team, 1963, 1964, 1966, 1967, 1971, 1973
NCAA Champion, 1961
Byron Nelson Tournament Champion, 1964, 1965, 1967, 1972, 1973, 1975
Lowest scoring average seven different years, 1962, 1964, 1965, 1972, 1973, 1974, 1975; runner-up for five years.
Biggest money winner seven times in 14 years, 1964, 1965, 1967, 1971, 1972, 1973, 1975; runner-up four times.

CONTENTS

PART 1:
FULL SWING
FUNDAMENTALS

HOW TO GRIP

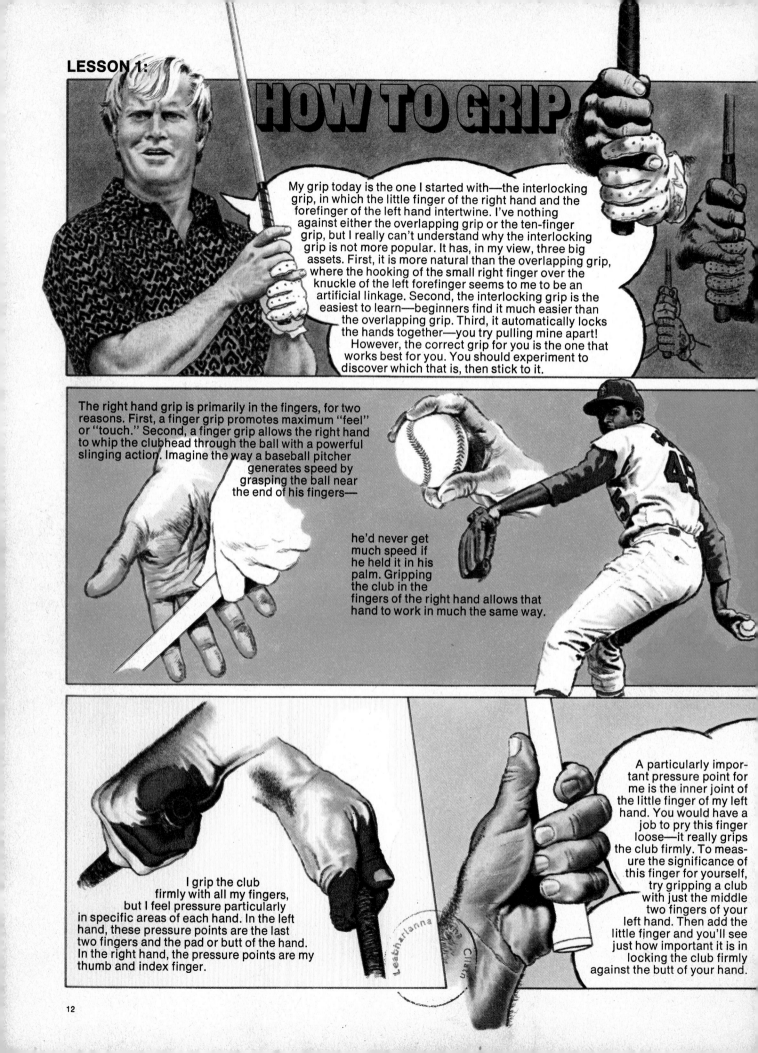

My grip today is the one I started with—the interlocking grip, in which the little finger of the right hand and the forefinger of the left hand intertwine. I've nothing against either the overlapping grip or the ten-finger grip, but I really can't understand why the interlocking grip is not more popular. It has, in my view, three big assets. First, it is more natural than the overlapping grip, where the hooking of the small right finger over the knuckle of the left forefinger seems to me to be an artificial linkage. Second, the interlocking grip is the easiest to learn—beginners find it much easier than the overlapping grip. Third, it automatically locks the hands together—you try pulling mine apart!
However, the correct grip for you is the one that works best for you. You should experiment to discover which that is, then stick to it.

The right hand grip is primarily in the fingers, for two reasons. First, a finger grip promotes maximum "feel" or "touch." Second, a finger grip allows the right hand to whip the clubhead through the ball with a powerful slinging action. Imagine the way a baseball pitcher generates speed by grasping the ball near the end of his fingers—

he'd never get much speed if he held it in his palm. Gripping the club in the fingers of the right hand allows that hand to work in much the same way.

I grip the club firmly with all my fingers, but I feel pressure particularly in specific areas of each hand. In the left hand, these pressure points are the last two fingers and the pad or butt of the hand. In the right hand, the pressure points are my thumb and index finger.

A particularly important pressure point for me is the inner joint of the little finger of my left hand. You would have a job to pry this finger loose—it really grips the club firmly. To measure the significance of this finger for yourself, try gripping a club with just the middle two fingers of your left hand. Then add the little finger and you'll see just how important it is in locking the club firmly against the butt of your hand.

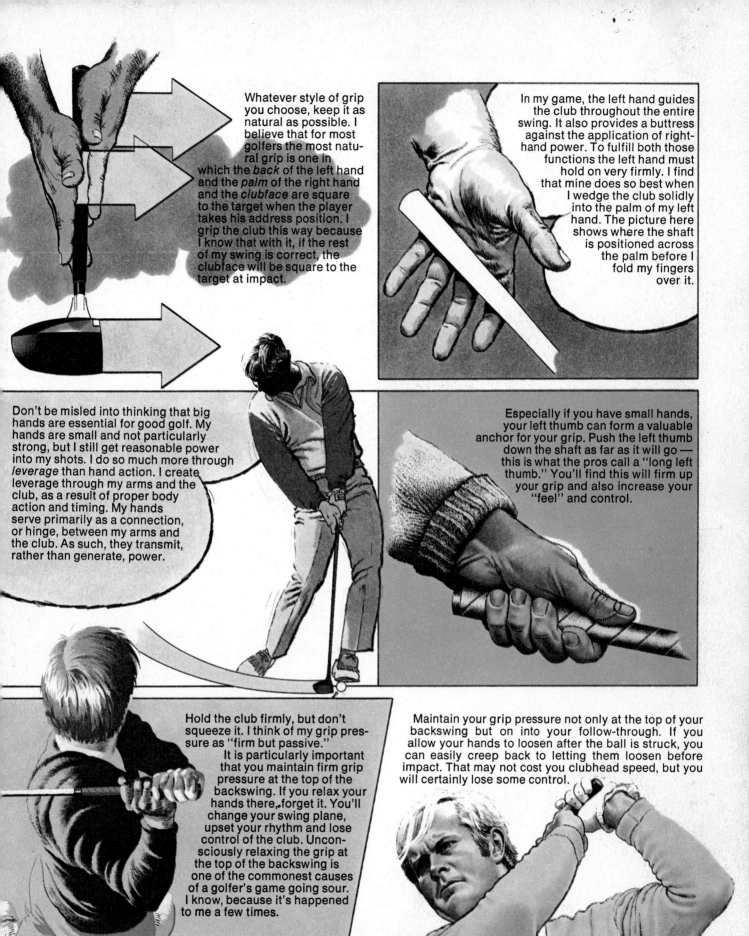

Whatever style of grip you choose, keep it as natural as possible. I believe that for most golfers the most natural grip is one in which the *back* of the left hand and the *palm* of the right hand and the *clubface* are square to the target when the player takes his address position. I grip the club this way because I know that with it, if the rest of my swing is correct, the clubface will be square to the target at impact.

In my game, the left hand guides the club throughout the entire swing. It also provides a buttress against the application of right-hand power. To fulfill both those functions the left hand must hold on very firmly. I find that mine does so best when I wedge the club solidly into the palm of my left hand. The picture here shows where the shaft is positioned across the palm before I fold my fingers over it.

Don't be misled into thinking that big hands are essential for good golf. My hands are small and not particularly strong, but I still get reasonable power into my shots. I do so much more through *leverage* than hand action. I create leverage through my arms and the club, as a result of proper body action and timing. My hands serve primarily as a connection, or hinge, between my arms and the club. As such, they transmit, rather than generate, power.

Especially if you have small hands, your left thumb can form a valuable anchor for your grip. Push the left thumb down the shaft as far as it will go — this is what the pros call a "long left thumb." You'll find this will firm up your grip and also increase your "feel" and control.

Hold the club firmly, but don't squeeze it. I think of my grip pressure as "firm but passive."
It is particularly important that you maintain firm grip pressure at the top of the backswing. If you relax your hands there, forget it. You'll change your swing plane, upset your rhythm and lose control of the club. Unconsciously relaxing the grip at the top of the backswing is one of the commonest causes of a golfer's game going sour. I know, because it's happened to me a few times.

Maintain your grip pressure not only at the top of your backswing but on into your follow-through. If you allow your hands to loosen after the ball is struck, you can easily creep back to letting them loosen before impact. That may not cost you clubhead speed, but you will certainly lose some control.

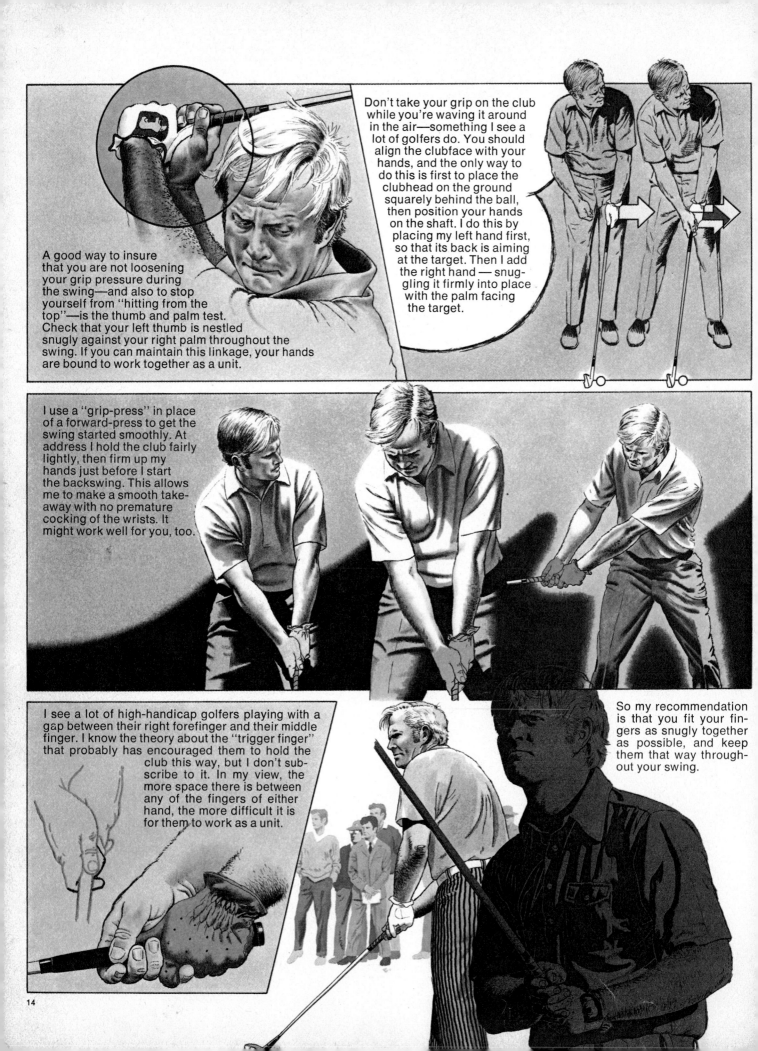

A good way to insure that you are not loosening your grip pressure during the swing—and also to stop yourself from "hitting from the top"—is the thumb and palm test. Check that your left thumb is nestled snugly against your right palm throughout the swing. If you can maintain this linkage, your hands are bound to work together as a unit.

Don't take your grip on the club while you're waving it around in the air—something I see a lot of golfers do. You should align the clubface with your hands, and the only way to do this is first to place the clubhead on the ground squarely behind the ball, then position your hands on the shaft. I do this by placing my left hand first, so that its back is aiming at the target. Then I add the right hand — snuggling it firmly into place with the palm facing the target.

I use a "grip-press" in place of a forward-press to get the swing started smoothly. At address I hold the club fairly lightly, then firm up my hands just before I start the backswing. This allows me to make a smooth take-away with no premature cocking of the wrists. It might work well for you, too.

I see a lot of high-handicap golfers playing with a gap between their right forefinger and their middle finger. I know the theory about the "trigger finger" that probably has encouraged them to hold the club this way, but I don't subscribe to it. In my view, the more space there is between any of the fingers of either hand, the more difficult it is for them to work as a unit.

So my recommendation is that you fit your fingers as snugly together as possible, and keep them that way throughout your swing.

Whichever way you choose to hold the club, always remember that the basic objective is firm unifying of the hands. The fewer the gaps between the fingers of each hand, and between the two hands themselves, the more your grip will function as a unit throughout the swing.

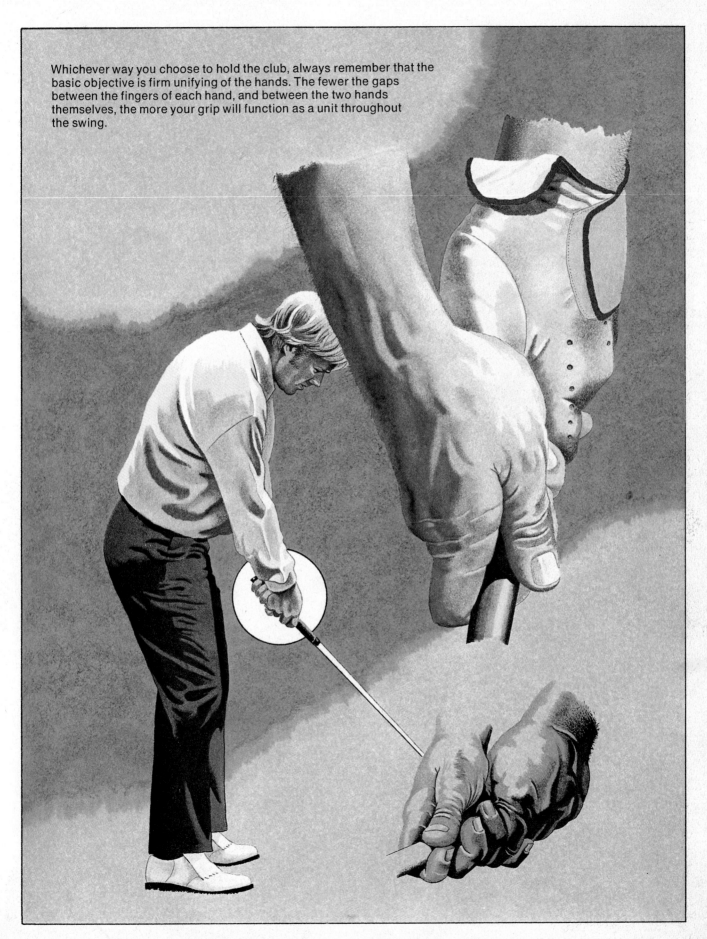

AIM, STANCE AND POSTURE

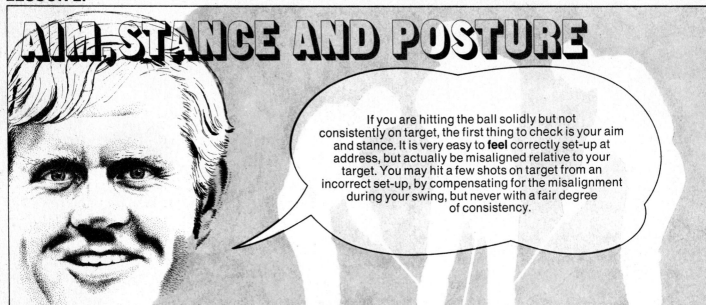

If you are hitting the ball solidly but not consistently on target, the first thing to check is your aim and stance. It is very easy to **feel** correctly set-up at address, but actually be misaligned relative to your target. You may hit a few shots on target from an incorrect set-up, by compensating for the misalignment during your swing, but never with a fair degree of consistency.

I never attempt to hit the ball dead straight. Thus, I don't personally set-up square. I don't align myself exactly parallel to the target line. For a fade I aim my clubface slightly right of target and align my torso slightly left. For a draw I aim the clubface slightly left of target and align my torso slightly right.

However, I believe that, until you become a very accomplished golfer, a "square" set-up as shown here—feet, hips and shoulders parallel to the target line—best enables you to swing the club along that line through impact.

If you've been consistently slicing or hooking the ball, it's a safe bet you're badly aligned, even though you may feel that you are "on target." So have your alignment periodically checked by your pro.

To me, the correct ball location for all shots under normal conditions is opposite the left heel. This is the point in the arc of my normal full swing at which the clubhead is traveling along the target line. If the ball were farther back, I would strike it while the club was still coming too much from inside the target line. If the ball were farther forward, I would contact it with the clubhead returning inside the target line—hitting, in effect, from out-to-in.

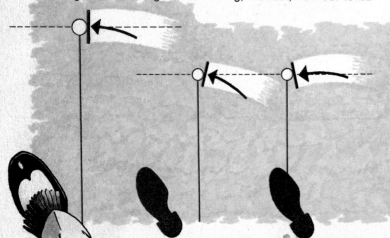

Address the ball off the center of the clubface—where you w to strike it. Addressing the ball near the toe or heel—as you sometimes see even good players do—makes no sense to me. just adds error to error by requiring a change in the swing to meet the ball squarely. Likewise, sole the club flat on the groun behind the ball—not up on its toe or heel. If you can't do that, either your address posture or the lie of your clubs is incorrect. Have both checked out by your pro.

It's a common—and fatal—mistake of many golfers to wait until they are set over the ball to determine their target. Always establish your target very clearly in your mind **before** you step up to the ball. You cannot aim correctly unless you select a specific target on which to align. Don't be vague. On shots where you're not going for the pin, pick out a marker on the ground or in the background that gives you a definite aiming point.

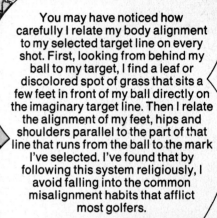

You may have noticed how carefully I relate my body alignment to my selected target line on every shot. First, looking from behind my ball to my target, I find a leaf or discolored spot of grass that sits a few feet in front of my ball directly on the imaginary target line. Then I relate the alignment of my feet, hips and shoulders parallel to the part of that line that runs from the ball to the mark I've selected. I've found that by following this system religiously, I avoid falling into the common misalignment habits that afflict most golfers.

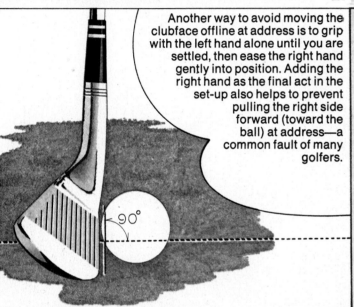

Another way to avoid moving the clubface offline at address is to grip with the left hand alone until you are settled, then ease the right hand gently into position. Adding the right hand as the final act in the set-up also helps to prevent pulling the right side forward (toward the ball) at address—a common fault of many golfers.

It's imperative that your clubface continues to face where you've originally aimed it as you complete your stance. Many golfers actually turn the clubface off-line, usually with the right hand, as they move into their final set-up position. To avoid that tendency I hold the club very lightly during the setting-up process, firming up my grip as the final movement before starting my backswing.

J McQueen

Your posture at address is very important because it controls both the plane of your swing and your balance. I believe your head should always be behind a line drawn vertically up from the ball. Your knees should be slightly flexed, and you should bend from the waist just far enough to allow your arms to hang in a natural and unrestricted fashion. Set your left arm reasonably straight and firm, so that it and the club form a relatively straight line from your left shoulder to the ball. Free your right arm of tension by letting it bend easily at the elbow. This will correctly set your right shoulder lower than your left shoulder, and your right side "under" your left.

STARTING YOUR SWING

I really couldn't tell you at what exact moment my backswing begins. My waggle, my "stationary press" (the firming of my grip), the slight turn of my head to the right and my takeaway are all so closely melded that they are almost a continuous movement. And that's the way I want it, because the very WORST way to start back is from a static, frozen or rigid position. If you do that, your swing is bound to be either jerky and uncoordinated or stiff and forced.

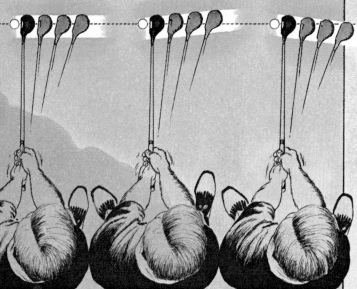

On a normal shot, I waggle the club back and forth along my target line — straight back and "through" the ball. If I am planning a definite fade, I waggle the clubhead on a slightly out-to-in path. If I intend to draw the shot, I waggle the club-head on an in-to-out line. I find such preliminary movements help reinforce my mental picture of the shot I'm about to play. They also "coach" my muscles into the desired pattern of movement.

As I waggle myself into position over the ball, I hold the club fairly loosely. Just before I start the backswing, I firm up my grip by pressing my hands together on the shaft once or twice. I call this a "stationary press," and I use it in place of the more common forward press, for a number of reasons.

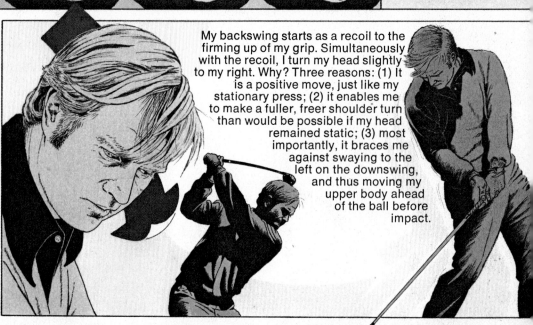

By firming up my hands as the final preparatory movement, I get a strong sense of AFFIRMATION of the coming swing throughout my body. This simple little device seems to alert all my muscles to the job at hand without tensing them in any way. Thus it has become a very critical part of my game, a preface to every shot I play. You should work to build a similarly strong "starter" into your game.

My backswing starts as a recoil to the firming up of my grip. Simultaneously with the recoil, I turn my head slightly to my right. Why? Three reasons: (1) It is a positive move, just like my stationary press; (2) it enables me to make a fuller, freer shoulder turn than would be possible if my head remained static; (3) most importantly, it braces me against swaying to the left on the downswing, and thus moving my upper body ahead of the ball before impact.

A little waggling of the club does a lot for me by keeping me "loose" in the final stages of setting up to the shot. I believe that the ideal waggle includes most of the elements present at the start of the backswing — which means a motion combining hands, arms, body and legs.

I have the feeling that my weight is moving back and forth, very slightly, as I waggle the club. This keeps my legs from becoming taut. The waggle itself serves the same function with my arms and wrists.

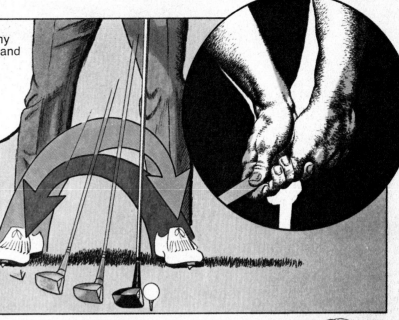

The forward press is used to a greater or lesser degree by most top golfers. Gary Player, for instance, kicks his right knee to the left. For many the forward press involves a slight move toward the target with the legs, hips and hands just before the backswing starts. This is certainly better than no press at all, but for me it is too variable a movement. If I used it I'd never be sure that I'd start back the same way every time. My firming up of the grip—my "stationary press"—has the same tension-easing purpose as the forward press. But to me it is a smaller and more contained movement.

J McQueen

A lot of good golfers make a similar turning of the head to the right at the start of the swing—Sam Snead is a notable example. Try it yourself, especially if you are coming "off" or "over" the ball on your downswing.

A factor to avoid if you try this move is letting your head sway laterally to the right as your backswing progresses. If that happens, as it does to a lot of golfers who follow the club away with their eyes, your swing arc will change and you will strike the ball inconsistently at best. I actually watch the clubhead move away myself, to check that it is doing so correctly. But I use side or peripheral vision to do so, not head movement.

I think that one of the most important takeaway rules concerns the action of the left side. Your entire left side must move together, or in "one piece," right from the outset if you're going to achieve power and consistency. In my own case, if there's a stronger muscular sensation or pressure in any other part of my body as I start the club back, I know I'm in trouble.

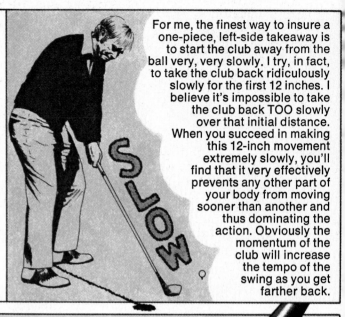

For me, the finest way to insure a one-piece, left-side takeaway is to start the club away from the ball very, very slowly. I try, in fact, to take the club back ridiculously slowly for the first 12 inches. I believe it's impossible to take the club back TOO slowly over that initial distance. When you succeed in making this 12-inch movement extremely slowly, you'll find that it very effectively prevents any other part of your body from moving sooner than another and thus dominating the action. Obviously the momentum of the club will increase the tempo of the swing as you get farther back.

The beginning of the backswing almost always "programs" the remainder of the swing. This being the case, here are some more factors that play a big part in my takeaway: (1) I swing the club straight back from the ball, without breaking my wrists, for as long as the turning of my shoulders and hips will allow, so that I may achieve the broadest possible swing arc. (2) I try to keep the clubface square to the target line for as long as possible, never turning my hands and wrists under to hold the clubface artificially on that line. (3) I try to keep my left arm and club in a straight line until the sheer momentum of the swinging clubhead causes my wrists to cock naturally.

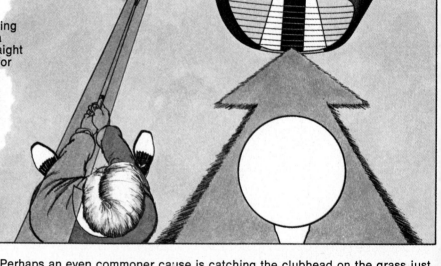

I feel the latter point is particularly relevant to club golfers, whom I often see drawing back with the clubhead lagging behind their hands. One cause of this is overly relaxed wrists at address (you might cure this with my "stationary press").

Perhaps an even commoner cause is catching the clubhead on the grass just as it starts back. I believe this comes from allowing the club to lie on the ground too heavily, or even pressing it down behind the ball at address.
To avoid any possibility of stubbing—and to promote smoothness—I start back with the clubhead just above the ground. If you find this difficult to do, at least be sure to ground it only very lightly.

However you choose to start the swing, make the initial movements—during the first 12 inches—as *smoothly* and *deliberately* as you possibly can, swinging rather than "taking" the club back. And keep the clubface looking at the ball until your body turn naturally moves it inside the target line.

BACKSWING TURN

My distance comes from leverage, my leverage comes from a full swing arc, and my full swing arc comes from a big body turn on the backswing. Most high-handicap golfers lack distance because, in place of a turn, they lift the club with their hands and arms. That's a lazy way to make a backswing and it results in an unacceptable shot. Other high-handicappers lack distance because, although they turn some parts of their body, they do so in a direction or in a sequence that fails to produce torsion, the necessary wind-up or coiling. They build no snap into the spring at the top. Let me give you the basics on which my backswing turn is built.

My right knee serves as an "insurance" anchor as the backswing progresses. It remains slightly flexed and slightly "kicked-in" toward the target. If my right knee straightened or crumpled, it would be impossible to "wind the spring" above it to full tension.

I start the club back with a one-piece movement of my whole left side, the left arm and club remaining in a straight line until the weight of the clubhead begins to cock my wrists as they reach about hip height. This one-piece action forces my shoulders to turn from the very beginning of the backswing and insures they will go on turning until its completion. Most weekend golfers cock their wrists early in the backswing, and as soon as they do their shoulders stop turning.

As my arms stretch and my shoulders turn, my hips also are forced to turn. I don't try to restrict that. I don't buy the modern theory about "keeping the hips still." The way I'm built, if my hips don't turn, neither will my shoulders. All I care about is that my hips don't turn ahead of my shoulders and that they don't turn farther than my shoulders.

I do not consciously cock my wrists at any point in the swing, because as soon as I do my shoulders would want to cop out and stop turning. What happens is that, in the final phase of the backswing, the weight of the clubhead naturally causes a hinging of the wrists.

J McQueen

First, although my head swivels to the right as I start back, the back of my neck stays in the same place throughout the backswing. This is my upper anchor—the fulcrum or pivotal point or hub of the swing. Any movement in it—up, down or sideways — would diminish the amount of torsion I can create in my body.

My lower anchors are my feet. I play from the *inside* of them, whereas most high-handicappers play from the outside of their feet. As the backswing develops, my weight rolls increasingly off the inside of my left foot onto the inside of my right foot. But it never goes *beyond* the inside of the right foot. That's another torsion-builder.

Throughout the early part of the backswing I stretch my left arm and the club as far away from the target as they will go while keeping my weight on the inside of my right foot and the back of my neck where it was at address. Later in the backswing I try to stick my arms through the clouds, stretching them as high as they will go without loosening my grip on the club. This again forces a full shoulder turn, and the result again is torsion.

This stretching of the arms and club produces what has been called my "flying right elbow." Actually, a flying right elbow is one that has been lifted and pointed behind the player at the top of his swing. At the top of my swing my right elbow points *downward*. So I don't really have a "flying right elbow," but an *extended* elbow. Without it, there'd be no way I could make the full left-arm stretch and shoulder turn I need to generate torsion.

At the top on a full drive, my shoulders have turned probably 110 degrees and my hips about 55 or 60 degrees. I feel stretched, coiled, wound-up, full of torsion and leverage—good and ready to send the ball on a nice long journey.

LESSON 5:

AT THE TOP

At the top of the backswing I am so coiled and stretched that it would be impossible for me to hold the position for more than a second or two. I have created so much torque in my body that the downswing *must* begin as a reflex action.

A lot of weekend golfers, whose golfing muscles aren't as well-trained as mine, might find it difficult to "wind the spring" this tight. But if you want power, full coiling at the top of the swing to the maximum of your physical capabilities should be one of your major goals.

One of the most critical angles in golf is the alignment of the club shaft at the top of the backswing. I want it to parallel my target line. If the shaft "crosses the line" — points right of target—I will hit too much from the inside and either hook or push the shot. If the shaft is "laid off"—points left of target—I will hit too much from the outside and either pull or slice the shot. Between 1968 and 1970 I fell into the habit of "crossing the line" repeatedly with very erratic results. Thus, today I repeatedly check the alignment of the shaft at the top of my swing to be sure it is pointing at my target.

How far should you swing back? It depends on your physique and your style of play. As long as you don't straighten your right knee, come way up on the toe of your left foot, or let go of the club, you can't swing too far back on full shots—even if, like some supple ladies, you dip the clubhead far past horizontal at the top.

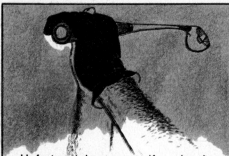

Unfortunately, many golfers develop a full swing in the worst possible way, by letting the club go loose in their hands at the top. This is usually the result of "lazy" body action, lifting the club with the hands and arms instead of turning the shoulders on the backswing. Another cause is too fast a backswing—yanking the club back so fast that the fingers can't control it at the top.

The best cure I know for letting go of the club is to maintain a uniformly firm grip pressure from take-away to top of swing, at the same time consciously snuggling the pad of the right thumb against the top of the left thumb. If you can get to the top with those two areas making contact, it is almost impossible to let go of the club.

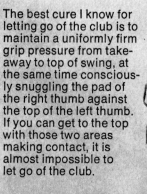

Should you pause at the top? I think you definitely should not. In fact, it would be impossible to do so the way I swing, because there really is no point in my action where the backswing stops and the downswing starts. As my arms reach their fullest extension and the weight of the clubhead causes my wrists to attain their maximum cocking, my legs and hips already have initiated the downswing.

In other words, the two halves of the swing meld together — my lower half starts the downswing as my top half completes the backswing. Any conscious attempt to pause at this point would destroy my balance and my tempo. To me, a better thought is "wait for the legs to work before the hands start down." The last thing I want to do is bring my backswing to a dead stop before my downswing starts.

Within those parameters, the fuller the swing the more powerful it is likely to be. In my own case, the club usually goes back just past horizontal on a full drive or fairway wood shot, progressively less as distance becomes secondary to direction.

At the top of the swing my weight is still on the inside of my feet, the best guarantee I know for not swaying while making the fullest possible turn. Because my right knee remains flexed, thus anchoring the action, I get the feeling that my weight is predominantly on my right foot, but there is actually still plenty on the inside of my left foot. On a full drive my left heel often lifts off the ground slightly at the top, but with the other clubs I try to keep it in contact with the ground throughout the swing.

My right elbow position at the top of my swing has caused comment throughout my career. As I've said before, my elbow doesn't "fly." To do that, it would have to point behind me. What it actually does is rise high in order to give me maximum arm extension going back. But at the completion of the backswing it points *down at the ground*.

If you lack power, forget that old maxim about tucking the right elbow into the side going back. Try my style. As long as the elbow points to the ground at the top and not behind you, letting it swing away from the body will help to increase both your body turn and your clubhead arc. Just be careful that in stretching your arms as you complete the swing you don't sway your head away from the target.

One of the great arguments in golf concerns the ideal alignment of the clubface at the top of the swing. Should it be "open" — toe pointing to the ground? Should it be "closed" — clubface looking skyward? Should it be "square"—aligned midway between "open" and "closed?" There is no simple answer. It depends on your physique, your grip, your style of swing and the type of shots you aim to hit.

In general, an open clubface at the top will result in an open clubface at the bottom, causing a slice. Conversely, a closed clubface at the top will result in a closed clubface at the bottom, creating a hook. But this is not an inviolate rule. Lee Trevino, for example, fades most of his shots from a closed position at the top by working the clubface from closed to open through the ball. Frank Beard, on the other hand, draws his shots by working the clubface from open to closed through the ball.

Since my basic shot is a fade, my ideal clubface position at the top is between open and square. But I don't actually think about the clubface at this point. Instead, I think of the flesh-and-blood factors that control the clubface angle here—my hands, wrists and arms.

With my type of grip, the clubface will be square at the top when my left hand and wrist are in line with my left forearm. If my left hand is more under the shaft—producing a concave bend at the wrist — the clubface will be more open. If my left hand is arched backward — producing a convex bend at the wrist — my clubface will be more closed.

I play best from the square position, not bad from the open position, and almost always poorly when I fall into a closed position. I think most other golfers have the same experience.

26

The tighter you can wind the upper half of your body against the resistance of your lower half, the more distance-producing leverage you will create. You cannot turn your shoulders too much or swing your arms too far back so long as you do not sway your body, stiffen your right knee, bend your left arm, or lose your grip.

STARTING DOWN

To me, the downswing is a reflex rather than a conscious action. Once you release the spring you've wound up on your backswing, there isn't enough time to direct your movements consciously. In the good golf swing the right downswing moves occur automatically in reaction to proper backswing moves. So if you have a faulty downswing, look at your set-up or backswing for the reasons.

Since I am a legs-and-body player, the accent in my downswing is almost entirely on foot, leg and hip action. My hands, arms and upper torso obviously do a lot of work, but they do it subconsciously. Compared to the action of my legs and hips, my hands and arms function passively on most full shots.

A major fault of the average golfer is starting the downswing with his hands and arms *before* his legs and hips have begun to work. Inevitably, this brings his shoulders into action too early, and his clubhead is thrown forward outside the target line, producing that weak pull-slice. Unfortunately, when they are made aware of these errors, most weekend golfers go to the other extreme. They will overuse their legs and hips and underuse their hands and arms.

As I see it, you can't hit too soon or too hard with your arms and hands *as long as you start the downswing with your legs and hips and continue to lead with your lower half through impact.* During the downswing I make no conscious effort to restrain my hands, arms or shoulders. I want them to move as freely and fast as possible, providing they *follow* my lower-body actions. In my book, "hitting from the top" is to be cured not by consciously decelerating hand and arm action but simply by increasing or accelerating leg and hip action.

Even when a golfer's legs are in passable shape, he'll often wreck his chance of using them correctly in the downswing by stiffening his right knee on the backswing. This is never an easy fault to cure, because it facilitates a lazy way to make a backswing turn. But it has to be cured before a player can correctly initiate the downswing with a lateral knee movement and a hip slide and turn toward the target.

Domination of the club by the right side is another downswing wrecker. The leading and controlling forces of the left side easily can be destroyed by a power play of the right hand, arm, hip or shoulder. With the exception of my right leg thrust, I try to use my right side as a follower, not a leader, throughout the downswing.

My downswing actually starts before my backswing is completed. The forward action begins in my feet. As the very first move of the downswing, while my arms are still swinging up, my left heel returns to earth and I begin to push hard off the inside of my right foot, throwing weight laterally to the *inside* of my left foot.

The effect of these actions is to move both my knees fast and forcefully in the direction of the shot. As this lateral knee slide develops, my hips — which have been sliding laterally along with my legs — begin to turn to the left, to clear a path for my arms to swing the club along the target line.

I am told these lateral actions are visually very pronounced in my game. They are certainly critical to my performance, and I regard the strong legs that make them possible my greatest asset. That is one of the reasons I keep active with tennis and other sports around home.

Do not fear that by leading the downswing with your legs and hips you'll prevent your wrists from uncocking in time to make square contact at impact. Correct downswing leg action builds such massive centrifugal force in the clubhead that your wrists will be forced to uncock as the clubface approaches the ball.

Most average golfers have problems learning to use their legs properly in the downswing. One reason is that their legs are often in poor shape from lack of exercise. If you want to improve your golf quickly, just try walking briskly instead of riding in a golf car.

One absolute downswing "must" whatever your golfing standard or type of swing: keep your head back behind the ball until well after impact. Swaying the head and upper body forward at the start of the downswing is one of the most common faults I see in the average amateur. Slide the knees and turn the hips . . . . but keep the head behind the ball!

PART 2: CRITICAL SWING FACTORS

LESSON 7:
EQUIPMENT

Although you can never "buy" a golf game, the better you become the more you will benefit from clubs that exactly suit your swing characteristics. How do you find them? The only certain way is by trial and error. That's why tour pros are so fond of hitting each other's clubs on the practice tee—especially drivers and wedges.

The higher priced a club, the better its raw materials and the more precise the shaping, assembling and finishing work that has gone into it. But that doesn't mean a lower-priced club won't work as well for you, especially if you're not yet quite ready to try for a pro tour card. I believe that mass-production techniques have reached such a point today that almost every club on the market has at least reasonable playability value. I also believe that beginners are better off starting with inexpensive clubs. It makes refitting as a player's game improves less painful on the pocket. The important thing in any club selection, however, is personal suitability—not price.

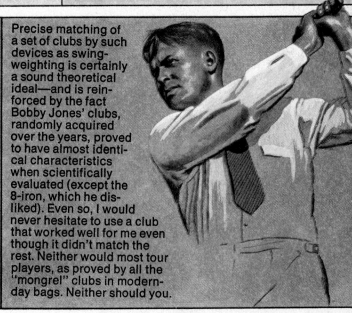

The feel of many modern sets of clubs is identified by swingweight, a concept relating the weight of the grip end of the club to its head weight. The objective is to provide uniformity of swing feel throughout each set. Generally speaking, the higher the swingweight designation the heavier the clubhead will feel in relation to the grip end as the club is swung.

It would take a book to analyze all the feel all performance nuances resulting from various combinations of shaft length and flex and grip and head weight. Basically, however, the stiffer the shaft, the greater the golfer's chance of delivering the clubface accurately to the ball, and thus the greater his percentage of shots in play; and the more flexible the shaft, the greater the potential clubhead speed and thus the greater the golfer's distance. But, when you get down to practicalities, the determining factors in selecting clubs must be your own strength, swing tempo and feel.

It's my belief that many golfers use clubs that are too heavy for them both in swingweight and dead weight, chiefly because a heavy club gives an unsophisticated golfer a sense of power. Yet clubhead *speed* is more important than clubhead weight in producing distance. Also, the lighter the club, the easier it is to control and the less tiring it is to keep on swinging. Keep these considerations in mind when selecting your next set.

Precise matching of a set of clubs by such devices as swing-weighting is certainly a sound theoretical ideal—and is reinforced by the fact Bobby Jones' clubs, randomly acquired over the years, proved to have almost identical characteristics when scientifically evaluated (except the 8-iron, which he disliked). Even so, I would never hesitate to use a club that worked well for me even though it didn't match the rest. Neither would most tour players, as proved by all the "mongrel" clubs in modern-day bags. Neither should you.

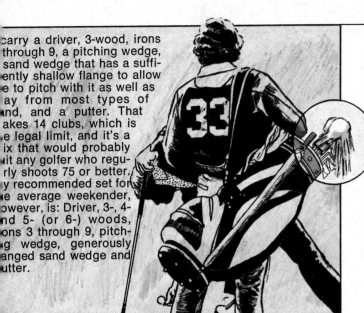

carry a driver, 3-wood, irons through 9, a pitching wedge, sand wedge that has a suffi-ently shallow flange to allow e to pitch with it as well as ay from most types of nd, and a putter. That akes 14 clubs, which is e legal limit, and it's a ix that would probably it any golfer who regu-rly shoots 75 or better. y recommended set for e average weekender, owever, is: Driver, 3-, 4-nd 5- (or 6-) woods, ons 3 through 9, pitch-g wedge, generously anged sand wedge and utter.

In choosing clubs, don't let cosmetic ap-pearances blind you to raw material, design and workmanship. For example, in check-ing a set of woods I always look to see that either the grain in persimmon or the laminations in bonded-wood heads are consistent and that the faces have proper bulge and roll (see illustration). With irons, consistency of lie, leading-edge configuration, face marking, gradation of offset, shaft-hosel bonding and grip thickness give clues to the care and precision with which the clubs have been manu-factured.

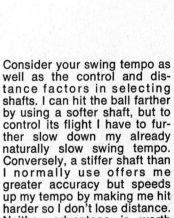

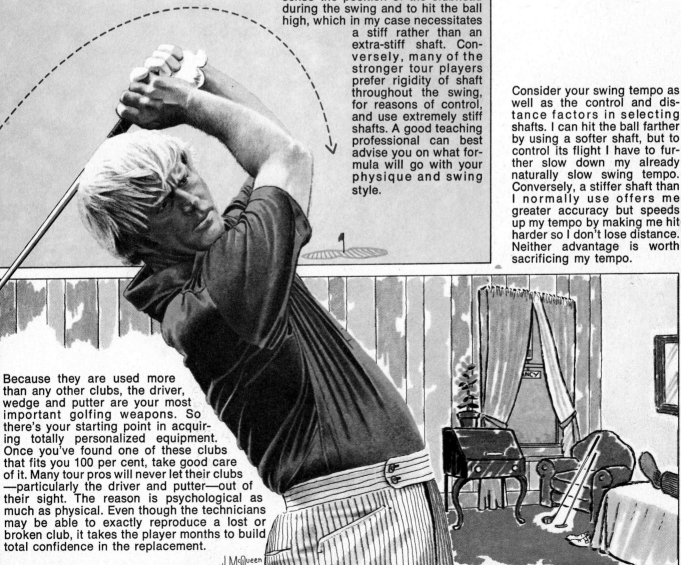

I, for example, like to be able to sense the position of the clubhead during the swing and to hit the ball high, which in my case necessitates a stiff rather than an extra-stiff shaft. Con-versely, many of the stronger tour players prefer rigidity of shaft throughout the swing, for reasons of control, and use extremely stiff shafts. A good teaching professional can best advise you on what for-mula will go with your physique and swing style.

Consider your swing tempo as well as the control and dis-tance factors in selecting shafts. I can hit the ball farther by using a softer shaft, but to control its flight I have to fur-ther slow down my already naturally slow swing tempo. Conversely, a stiffer shaft than I normally use offers me greater accuracy but speeds up my tempo by making me hit harder so I don't lose distance. Neither advantage is worth sacrificing my tempo.

Because they are used more than any other clubs, the driver, wedge and putter are your most important golfing weapons. So there's your starting point in acquir-ing totally personalized equipment. Once you've found one of these clubs that fits you 100 per cent, take good care of it. Many tour pros will never let their clubs —particularly the driver and putter—out of their sight. The reason is psychological as much as physical. Even though the technicians may be able to exactly reproduce a lost or broken club, it takes the player months to build total confidence in the replacement.

J McQueen

If you're a serious golfer, it's worth a maximum effort to search out the club specifications that suit you best. Trial and error is the only certain way. The driver, wedge and putter are the most critical clubs because they are used so often. Touring pros are forever trying each other's clubs—especially these three—in search of their perfect tools.

The lie of your clubs—the angle between clubhead and hosel —is vital. This is because you always want to return the clubface to the ball at impact just as you set the clubface at address. If the heel of the club is off the ground at address, chances are the toe will catch the ground and cause the clubface to open as the ball is struck. Conversely, if the toe of the club is off the ground at address, chances are the clubface will close as the heel strikes the ground first. So seek clubs that rest flat on the ground when you assume your normal address posture.

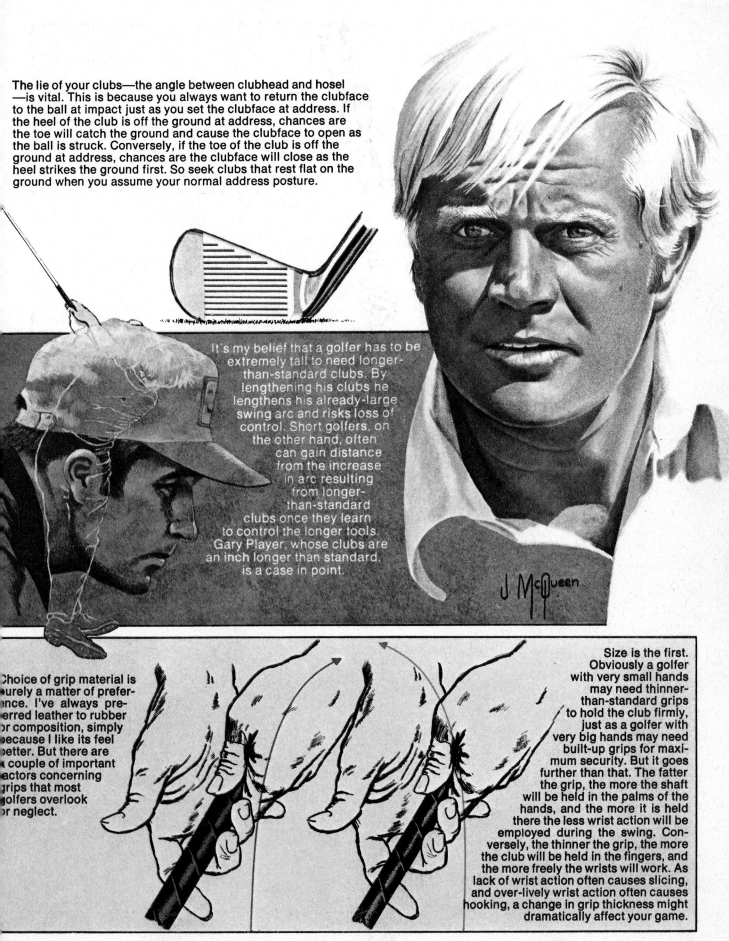

It's my belief that a golfer has to be extremely tall to need longer-than-standard clubs. By lengthening his clubs he lengthens his already-large swing arc and risks loss of control. Short golfers, on the other hand, often can gain distance from the increase in arc resulting from longer-than-standard clubs once they learn to control the longer tools. Gary Player, whose clubs are an inch longer than standard, is a case in point.

J McQueen.

Choice of grip material is surely a matter of preference. I've always preferred leather to rubber or composition, simply because I like its feel better. But there are a couple of important factors concerning grips that most golfers overlook or neglect.

Size is the first. Obviously a golfer with very small hands may need thinner-than-standard grips to hold the club firmly, just as a golfer with very big hands may need built-up grips for maximum security. But it goes further than that. The fatter the grip, the more the shaft will be held in the palms of the hands, and the more it is held there the less wrist action will be employed during the swing. Conversely, the thinner the grip, the more the club will be held in the fingers, and the more freely the wrists will work. As lack of wrist action often causes slicing, and over-lively wrist action often causes hooking, a change in grip thickness might dramatically affect your game.

The second grip factor concerns condition. Time and again in pro-ams I come across golfers whose leather grips are slick and dried-out, or whose rubber grips are as hard as the faces of their clubs. Holding onto the club firmly throughout the swing becomes almost impossible when the grip is in this condition, although it can be cured in the case of leather with conditioning oil and in the case of rubber or composition by soap, water and a scrubbing brush. When you're conditioning your grips, it might also be a good idea to do a little grooming of the heads. Dirt-encrusted clubfaces definitely influence the behavior of the ball, usually badly, which is why tour caddies so meticulously clean players' clubs after each shot. There is also something psychologically unsettling about looking down at a muck-covered clubface.

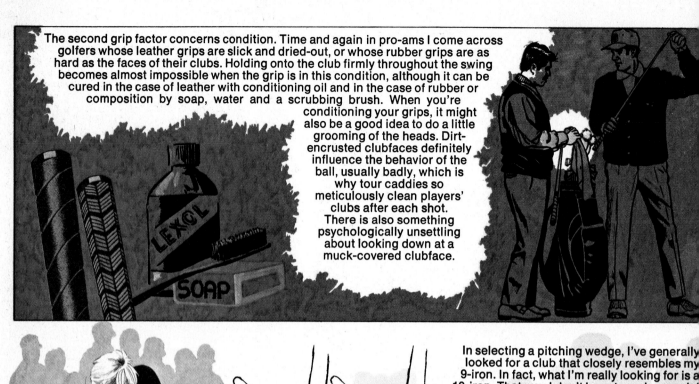

In selecting a pitching wedge, I've generally looked for a club that closely resembles my 9-iron. In fact, what I'm really looking for is a 10-iron. That way I don't have to make special swing adjustments every time I'm called on to play a wedge shot. The sand wedge has given me more trouble than any other single club primarily because I want to have my cake and eat it—have sufficient "bounce" with a rounded flange to enable me to play from all types of sand, yet not so much bounce that I can't pitch from grass. What I usually have settled for is a club similar to a dual-purpose wedge. But the golfer who has trouble in traps would do better, I believe, with more "bounce"—in other words, a deeply protruding flange which will reduce the tendency to bury the clubhead in the sand.

In choosing a ball, do some experimenting with different constructions. In the days when balls all were made basically from the same materials in the same way, they all flew pretty much alike. Today, the differences in flight characteristics arising from varying materials, construction techniques and dimple configurations allow a golfer who hits the ball too low to "buy" extra height, and the golfer who hits too high to "buy" lower shots. Take advantage of all opportunities in your selection of equipment.

Often a golfer suffering from a quick or jerky stroke will benefit from a heavy putter. A golfer who strokes too hesitantly or tends to decelerate through impact will benefit from a lighter putter. Playing the wide variety of green speeds we encounter on the tour, I find I am best served by a medium-weight club.

Irrespective of grip size or condition, many golfers have trouble hanging onto the club throughout the swing, especially with the left hand. If that's your problem, and you don't already use a glove, then get one. It's the greatest aid to secure gripping that you're allowed under the rules. It's also a way of preventing the blisters and calluses that would surely develop on a gloveless hand from the practice you should do.

Long irons are not all that hard to play if you can avoid letting them mentally terrorize you into a state of muscular paralysis. You swing them more like a 3-wood than a wedge—in other words, sweep rather than punch the ball. But there's no doubt that the 4- and 5-woods are much easier to handle than the 2- and 3-irons for most golfers, while doing basically the same job. In making your decision between the two, consider how often you are required to play long shots from the rough. The well-lofted woods will generally get you out reasonably effectively, whereas the less-lofted irons almost never will. That's why Lee Trevino, one of the straightest players in golf history, often carries a 6-wood on courses where fairways are narrow and the hay deep.

Choosing a putter is like finding a wife—entirely a matter of personal taste. I've used the same standard-length, flange-style blade, upright putter with a leather grip almost all my life. The only exceptional thing about it is that it is extremely well-balanced and allows me to stroke positively but fluidly. If you can find a putter that seems to swing smoothly and in balance while allowing you to strike the ball without extra effort, then hang onto it for dear life.

Probably the most important characteristic of a putter beyond its swinging balance is its lie. If you putt best standing a good distance from the ball, you will need a flat-lying club to be able to sole the blade without the toe sticking up. Conversely, if you stand close to the ball as I do—primarily so that I may set my eyes directly over the ball—then you will need a club with an upright lie.

What ball compression should you use? I personally use high-compression (100) balls most of the year, first because I can best achieve the flight characteristics I seek with a "hard" ball, and second because I believe a high-compression ball hit solidly goes farther than a low-compression ball in any conditions. But there's a mental factor here that you should consider: the effect of impact feel (stoniness vs. resilience) and "click" on your psyche. If a medium- or low-compression ball feels and sounds best, then the resulting confident shotmaking approach is going to be far more valuable to you than any slight additional distance you might get from a harder ball.

HOW TO SHAPE YOUR SHOTS

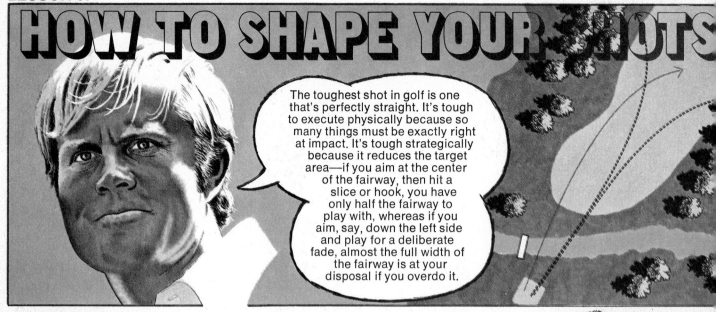

The toughest shot in golf is one that's perfectly straight. It's tough to execute physically because so many things must be exactly right at impact. It's tough strategically because it reduces the target area—if you aim at the center of the fairway, then hit a slice or hook, you have only half the fairway to play with, whereas if you aim, say, down the left side and play for a deliberate fade, almost the full width of the fairway is at your disposal if you overdo it.

I like to fade the ball most of the time, because control is a bigger problem for me than distance. If I were a shorter hitter, I might well have grown up favoring a draw. But, because power was not my problem even as a boy, my coach, Jack Grout, taught me to regard the fade as my basic "shape." I may, however, turn my game around and draw the ball for certain courses or conditions.

A big factor in Grout's reasoning was height of the shot. Because of spin characteristics, it is easier to hit a high fade than a high draw. Grout believed one of the major factors separating the great players from the rest was their ability to hit high, soft-landing long irons into tight targets. Bobby Jones was his favorite example. I agree with Jack 100 per cent.

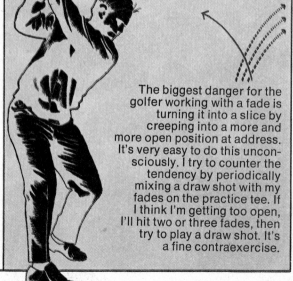

I believe the worst thing a golfer can do when trying to fade the ball is to try to cut the ball by swinging outside-in across the target line. First, a deliberate out-to-in swing is unnatural and contrived and therefore unreliable. Second, if you combine an out-to-in swing path with aiming left and an open clubface at address, you're almost certain to hit a big slice.

The biggest danger for the golfer working with a fade is turning it into a slice by creeping into a more and more open position at address. It's very easy to do this unconsciously. I try to counter the tendency by periodically mixing a draw shot with my fades on the practice tee. If I think I'm getting too open, I'll hit two or three fades, then try to play a draw shot. It's a fine contraexercise.

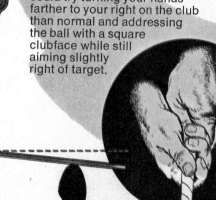

My method of drawing the ball is equally simple. All I do is aim a little to the right of target, close the clubface slightly, and then swing normally. If this doesn't work for you—and remember, it won't without practice—you could try turning your hands farther to your right on the club than normal and addressing the ball with a square clubface while still aiming slightly right of target.

For both these reasons I have never tried to hit the ball dead straight. Neither does any other golfer on the pro tour. Probably the majority of tour players draw the ball from right to left on their full shots. Others — especially the more powerful players—prefer to fade the ball from left to right. A few — the most skillful shotmakers — alternate between a draw and a fade depending on each particular shot situation.

Whatever your level of skill, I believe you'll score better if you adopt a policy of bending your shots instead of trying to hit them straight.

In choosing your shot "shape," give thought to the following: **1.** A fade gives you more control than a draw, because a faded ball backspins more, flies higher, breaks less sharply, lands more softly and stops quicker than a drawn ball. A draw gives you more distance than a fade, because a drawn ball flies lower, lands faster, and runs farther. **2.** If a fade turns into a slice, it will reduce your distance severely. If a draw turns into a hook it will often run into severe trouble. **3.** Fading the ball requires more technical ability than drawing the ball. **4.** Golf is simplest and easiest when you play *with,* rather than *against,* your natural tendencies —especially under pressure.

To fade the ball, the clubface at impact must face very slightly to the right of your clubhead path. To draw the ball, the clubface at impact must face very slightly to the left of your clubhead path. These are your basic impact objectives, whether you try to achieve a fade or draw.

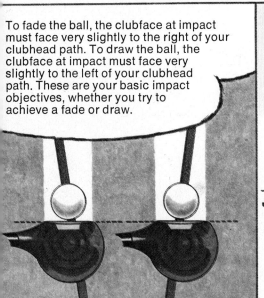

I'm not hot on many of the methods commonly prescribed for deliberately fading or drawing the ball. They're too complicated—they give you too many things to think about during the swing. I believe the way I fade the ball is the easiest and simplest way to do it (but that doesn't mean you'll master it without practice). All I do is align my body slightly left of the target at address, open the clubface a little, and then swing normally.

For me it's that simple, but if my method doesn't work for you, try this technique. Grip the club with both your hands turned farther to your left than normal, aim left, keep the clubface square at address, then swing normally.

The thing *not* to do in trying to develop a controlled draw is to deliberately swing inside-out across the target line. Again, this action is unnatural and therefore unreliable. If you do succeed, you'll hit a howling big hook.

The pitfall golfers who draw the ball must avoid is developing a hook by aiming too far right at address and swinging too flat. Again, a good way to guard against this is to periodically inject some fades into your practice sessions.

Whether you choose to fade or draw —and you *should* choose one or the other over the straight ball—avoid complicating the job. Make the *minimum* adjustments necessary —through experimenting on the practice tee—to shape the shot as you desire while still hitting it solidly with a natural, uncontrived swing.

SWING PLANE

The basic element that determines a golfer's sw[ing] plane is his physical stature combined with [his] address posture. The more a golfer bends over [the] ball from the waist at address, and/or the close[r he] sets his hands to his body, the more upright [he] naturally tends to swing. Similarly, a short pla[yer] will swing flatter than a tall player, simply beca[use] his lack of height in relation to the length of [the] clubshaft forces him to stand farther from the b[all.] You really should make no conscious determ[ina-]tion to swing flat or upright.

There are two more reasons why I favor a comparatively upright swing. First, the more upright your swing, the more backspin you will apply to the ball, the higher you will hit it and the quicker you will stop it. Second, my basic shot is a fade, and the more upright the plane, the easier it is to fade the ball from left to right and the more difficult to draw it from right to left.

But, a warning. If you see merits in a m[ore] upright plane, be sure you marry it to a la[rge] arc by maintaining full extension of the [left] arm and making a full shoulder turn go[ing] back. An "upright" swing that is the re[sult] simply of picking up the club with the ha[nds,] wrists and arms is useless.

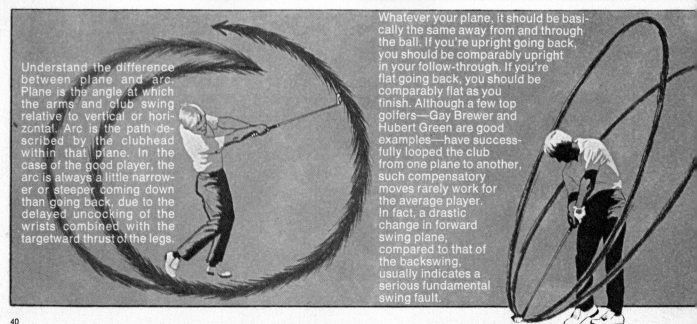

Understand the difference between plane and arc. Plane is the angle at which the arms and club swing relative to vertical or horizontal. Arc is the path described by the clubhead within that plane. In the case of the good player, the arc is always a little narrower or steeper coming down than going back, due to the delayed uncocking of the wrists combined with the targetward thrust of the legs.

Whatever your plane, it should be basically the same away from and through the ball. If you're upright going back, you should be comparably upright in your follow-through. If you're flat going back, you should be comparably flat as you finish. Although a few top golfers—Gay Brewer and Hubert Green are good examples—have successfully looped the club from one plane to another, such compensatory moves rarely work for the average player. In fact, a drastic change in forward swing plane, compared to that of the backswing, usually indicates a serious fundamental swing fault.

Theoretically, at least, the ideal swing plane would be vertical—like a pendulum—in that the club would never deviate from the target line. On the other hand, there is something to be said for the ultimately flat swing plane, i.e., horizontal, in that the club would always make contact exactly at ball level.

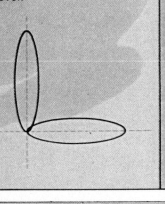

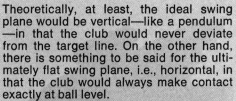

Ever since my amateur days, people have commented on my "flying right elbow." Actually, my elbow does not "fly." To do so it would have to point behind me at the top of the swing, whereas it actually points down to the ground. But the elbow at the top is certainly well away from my body, and I defy anyone to achieve a full arc on an upright plane without getting into a similar position. The important point is not so much the elbow position at the top. Rather, it is the elbow's movement back in close to the right side in response to the downswing being initiated by the targetward thrust of the legs.

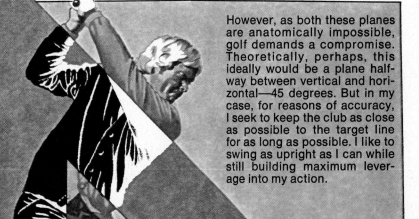

However, as both these planes are anatomically impossible, golf demands a compromise. Theoretically, perhaps, this ideally would be a plane halfway between vertical and horizontal—45 degrees. But in my case, for reasons of accuracy, I seek to keep the club as close as possible to the target line for as long as possible. I like to swing as upright as I can while still building maximum leverage into my action.

Many golfers seem to think they need to make a conscious effort to change the plane of the swing to suit certain clubs or achieve particular shots. Not so. The plane will change slightly with each club, becoming more upright as the club shortens and the golfer is obliged to stand closer to the ball. But the swing's basic configuration remains the same for all clubs and all normal shots. Only when you're under a tree branch or are similarly restricted do you need to attempt consciously to modify your "natural" plane.

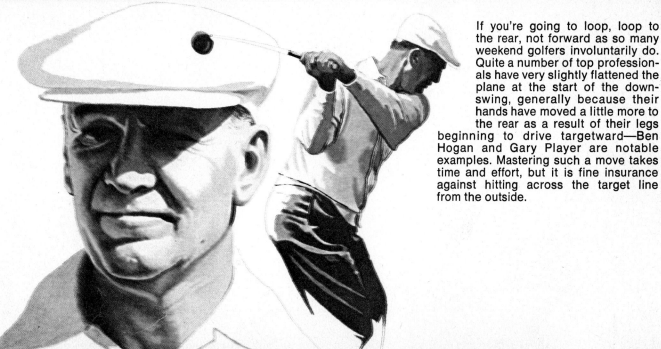

If you're going to loop, loop to the rear, not forward as so many weekend golfers involuntarily do. Quite a number of top professionals have very slightly flattened the plane at the start of the downswing, generally because their hands have moved a little more to the rear as a result of their legs beginning to drive targetward—Ben Hogan and Gary Player are notable examples. Mastering such a move takes time and effort, but it is fine insurance against hitting across the target line from the outside.

LESSON 10:
THE HEAD

The head is the fulcrum of the golf swing. As such it had better stay steady, if not absolutely stock-still, from the start back until well into the follow-through. All kinds of golfing evils stem from head movement. Here are three of the worst. 1. Midswing changes in arc and plane, causing every kind of mis-hit and mis-directed shot imaginable. 2. Variations of eye-alignment, causing incorrect visual relationship to the target line. 3. Loss of balance, causing dissipation of clubhead speed before impact.

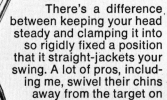

There's a difference between keeping your head steady and clamping it into so rigidly fixed a position that it straight-jackets your swing. A lot of pros, including me, swivel their chins away from the target on their backswings, and most good players allow the momentum of the follow-through to swivel their heads toward the target. Also, the camera has revealed that there is a slight backward and downward movement of the head during the forward swing of many fine golfers. As long as they are slight, these movements are permissible —and may even help eliminate rigidity and tension. It's sway and lift that you must guard against.

If you feel you have head-movement problems, practicing with a flat-footed swing could solve them. Keeping both feet firmly on the ground while hitting, say, 5-iron shots will help you keep your head steady by minimizing body action. The key to this flat-footed action, incidentally, is a rolling action of the ankles — inward with the left ankle on the backswing and inward with the right ankle on the through-swing.

If that doesn't work, probably the only way you'll stop your head movement is to think hard about holding it steady, which may well take an exaggerated effort at first. When practicing, try to complete the swing without lifting your head or letting your eyes move off the ball's location. This will force you into an abbreviated finish, but the resulting "feel" of a steady head ultimately will carry over into your normal swing.

There's another way a moving head can sabotage good swing form, and it's one not often mentioned by teaching professionals. To develop clubhead speed you must create leverage, and to create leverage you must turn and coil your upper body against the resistance of your lower body on the backswing. Any head movement can only weaken and distort this vital coiling action, thus costing you distance if not direction.

One of the best "head men" in the history of golf is Arnold Palmer. However violently he attacks the ball — and Arnie sure does *attack* a golf ball — his head stays put until the sheer force of his follow-through pulls it up well after the ball is on its way. Arnold, as I did, spent endless hours as a youngster practicing keeping his head steady. Even today he frequently checks himself in this area. I believe his ability to hold his fulcrum steady has often saved his game when some element of his swing was out of gear.

The old maxim "keep your eye on the ball" is sound, in the sense that it is difficult to hit an object you can't see. But don't take it for granted that, by keeping your eye on the ball, you are holding your head steady. I can sway my head two feet to either side and still look at the ball.

A simple way to check whether your head is moving is to watch your shadow when practice-swinging on a sunny day. Get the sun directly behind you, align the edge of your head shadow with a mark on the grass, then swing at a tee or a weed while watching your shadow. I often do this if I feel my topknot is jumping around.

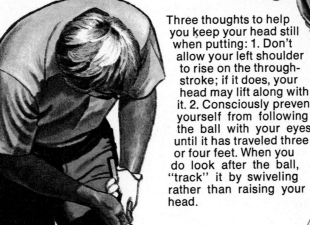

Anytime you don't accelerate the club through the ball with your arms there'll be a tendency to move your upper body (and thus your head) toward the target. Over-swinging going back is a prime cause of quitting coming down. "Measure" your backswing to the distance of your shot, then accelerate the clubhead through the ball with your arms as the shoulders move under and past a steady head.

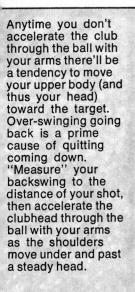

Three thoughts to help you keep your head still when putting: 1. Don't allow your left shoulder to rise on the through-stroke; if it does, your head may lift along with it. 2. Consciously prevent yourself from following the ball with your eyes until it has traveled three or four feet. When you do look after the ball, "track" it by swiveling rather than raising your head.

LESSON 11:
FOOTWORK

Proper footwork begins at address. Your stance must be narrow enough to allow you to move with ease, yet wide enough to provide a stable base for some fairly violent actions, especially with the longer clubs. In my case, this happy medium is achieved when I set the inside of my heels apart about the width of my shoulders for wooden club shots, gradually narrowing the stance as the clubs shorten until my heels are about six inches apart for a short wedge shot.

My left-foot positioning at address is the same for every club — about 30 degrees left of square. The purpose of this toeing out — which I think every golfer needs — is to facilitate free and easy left-side clearance during the down-and-through swing. So important is it in my case that, when I really need a big drive, I'll often open up my left foot to about 45 degrees, thereby guaranteeing maximum uncoiling of my hips through impact.

We hear theories today about distributing more weight on the right side than on the left at address. They're not for me. For the sake of comfort, balance and stability, I want my weight at address evenly divided not only between both feet but between the balls and heels of both feet. However, I do incline my legs slightly toward the target at address by pushing slightly toward my left side off the inside of my right foot (both ball and heel). If you try this, don't overdo it to the point where you unwittingly tilt your body forward of the ball.

Certainly, my left heel raises from the ground at the completion of the backswing with every club from the driver to the 3-iron. And my right heel comes off the ground through impact on all full shots. But such lifting is the *effect* of body coiling going back and of leg thrust coming down, never the *cause* of these moves. Allowing the left heel to rise quickly and high during the backswing is sometimes the only way an elderly or heavy-set golfer can assure a full body turn. If that's your medicine, the key fault to avoid is an involuntary raising of the head in sympathy with the heel lift. Such head movement results in a change of arc that will cause either a topped or "thin" shot if you stay up or "fat" contact if you dip coming down.

Because I play every shot with the ball positioned opposite my left heel, I move only my right foot in widening or narrowing my stance. If you have a problem maintaining a constant ball position, this technique would quickly solve it.

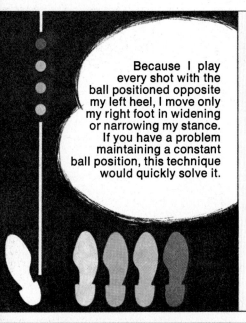

The angle of your feet at address has great bearing on both balance and motion during the swing. Setting the right foot square (at right angles) to the target line—as I do for most iron shots—limits hip and shoulder turn and is a good safeguard against over-swinging, especially for the supple golfer. The player who has difficulty making a full enough body turn, however, would be better off angling the right foot five to 10 degrees away from the target—as I do when going for the fullest possible turn with the driver or 3-wood.

90°

Jack Grout disciplined me many years ago to develop a rolling action of the ankles, rather than a lifting of the heels. It's one of the biggest favors he ever did me. Going back, the left foot rolls progressively onto its inside edge in response to the pull on the legs created by the upper-body turn. Coming down, I push off with an increasing roll onto the inside edge of my right foot as my leg/hip action transfers my weight onto my left side. Through the ball, my leg action, combined with the right-foot thrusting, also causes a rolling of the left foot toward the target. At the end of the follow-through I feel as though I'm carrying 95 per cent of my weight on the outside of my left foot.

It is important to this type of footwork — and to good over-all swing form—to retain a pre-ponderance of weight on the inside of the right foot during the backswing. Often I use a conscious shift of weight to the inside of my right foot as the initiating backswing "feel." As long as my right knee remains slightly flexed, I am certain to get the club back by turning and coiling, rather than swaying my body laterally—a major backswing fault of high handicappers.

lowing the right heel to ise prematurely coming own is one of the more ommon causes of spinning e entire body during the ownswing, instead of rusting the knees and hips terally toward the target. e result is that old familiar er-and-out action of the oulders, leading to an t-to-in clubhead route d a sliced or pulled shot.

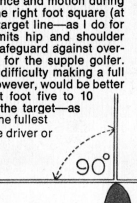

The finest practice I know for developing correct foot action is hitting with the feet close together, concen-trating on the rolling action of the ankles I've described in this lesson. Use a 5-iron, make a smooth three-quarter swing, and never let either heel raise off the ground. You'll be surprised what a couple of hours of this will do for your tempo, not to mention your over-all swing form.

LESSON 12:
THE ARMS

To swing a golf club smoothly, fluidly and on the fullest possible arc, your arms must be allowed to move freely in response to your shoulder, hip and leg action. To achieve that freedom, your arms must be in a relaxed and natural position at address. Avoid any posture that creates muscular rigidity, especially in your forearms. Tension in the forearms—often the product of too tight a grip—will severely restrict your upper-body turn by creating tension in your shoulders.

An important function of the arms at address is to measure your distance from the ball, again with the object of reproducing the ideal impact position. If the arms are too snug to the body at address, chances are there will be insufficient space for them to flow freely past it at impact. Over-extension of the arms at address, on the other hand, often forces a player to lurch his body forward on the downswing in order to reach the ball. Strike a happy medium—which I obtain by allowing my left arm and the clubshaft to dip slightly below a direct line from the clubhead to my left shoulder.

If you like to waggle—and most tour golfers find a couple of waggles indispensable both to minimizing muscular tension at address and making a smooth takeaway—beware of bending your left arm as you do so. A bent left arm during the waggle often leads to a bent left arm during the backswing. The longer you can maintain an unbroken line from the clubhead to your left shoulder during the backswing, the wider your arc will be and the more your shoulders will be forced to turn. Firmness—but not rigidity—at your left elbow and wrist is the key to maintaining that unbroken line.

Bending the left arm at the start of the downswing is a major malady among handicap golfers, and a fault I have to continually guard against in my own game. Results are a distortion of plane, a dissipation of leverage (and thus power) and a disastrously steep angle of attack on the ball — plus, usually, a collapsed left side at impact. In short, it is one of the most destructive moves a golfer can make.

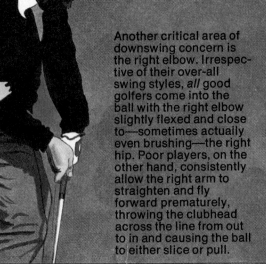

Another critical area of downswing concern is the right elbow. Irrespective of their over-all swing styles, *all* good golfers come into the ball with the right elbow slightly flexed and close to—sometimes actually even brushing—the right hip. Poor players, on the other hand, consistently allow the right arm to straighten and fly forward prematurely, throwing the clubhead across the line from out to in and causing the ball to either slice or pull.

Forcing the arms into unnatural positions at address has the same effect. So don't contort yourself to achieve some contrived alignment of your arms as you set up to the ball. Simply let them hang freely from your shoulders, with the elbows pointing in the same direction as when you stand with your arms at your sides.

In the final moments of addressing the ball, I like to feel that my left arm is firm enough to form a straight line with the shaft from the head of the club to my left shoulder without being rigid. The feeling I seek in my right arm is one of "softness," deriving from a slight bend at the elbow. This also has the effect of positioning the right arm slightly "under" the left. Thus set up, I am properly mirroring the position that I seek at impact.

Golfers of old maintained that the upper part of the right arm should never move away from the side during the backswing, and you'll find quite a few modern teachers supporting that view. If they're right, I'm in big trouble — because my right arm moves well away from my side, and pronouncedly behind me, on every full swing! There's no way I could achieve the width of arc and fullness of shoulder turn I seek without that happening. But a caution: *if you go for my kind of maximum extension, do it with your left arm in command,* keeping the right soft and submissive so that the elbow points *down,* never out, as you reach the top.

A big arc is the bedrock of my game, and to achieve it I cultivate a definite feeling of reaching for the sky with my left arm as I complete the backswing. As long as you guard against raising or swaying your head, or loosening your grip on the club, I believe a similar sensation would add width of arc, and thus power, to your drives.

J McQueen

The accuracy and power that result from maximum extension through the ball have always encouraged me to develop a feeling of keeping my left arm straight as long as I possibly can after impact—in fact, until it is forced by the sheer momentum of the club to break well into the follow-through. Such extension "through the ball" is the best insurance I know against both decelerating the club before impact and premature wrist-rolling —the one diminishing distance and the other distorting direction. Strong leg action, leading to full clearance of the hips to make room for the arms to swing past the body, is essential to achieve maximum arm extension. If you feel your arms are failing you through impact, the thing to work on is actually your lower-body action.

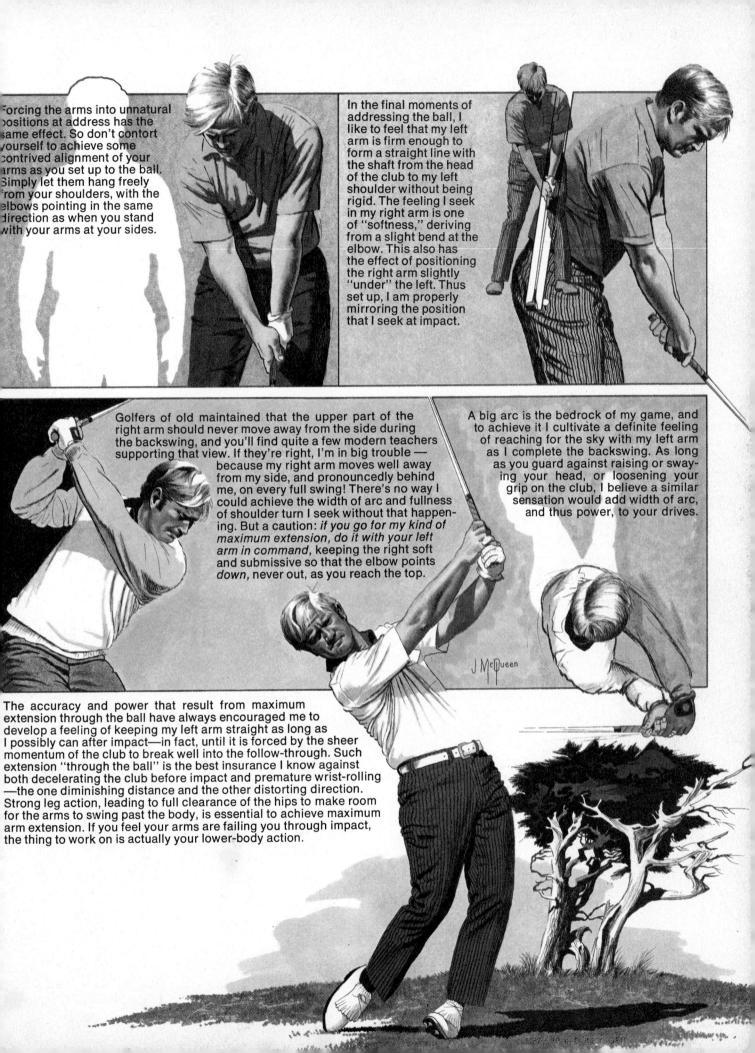

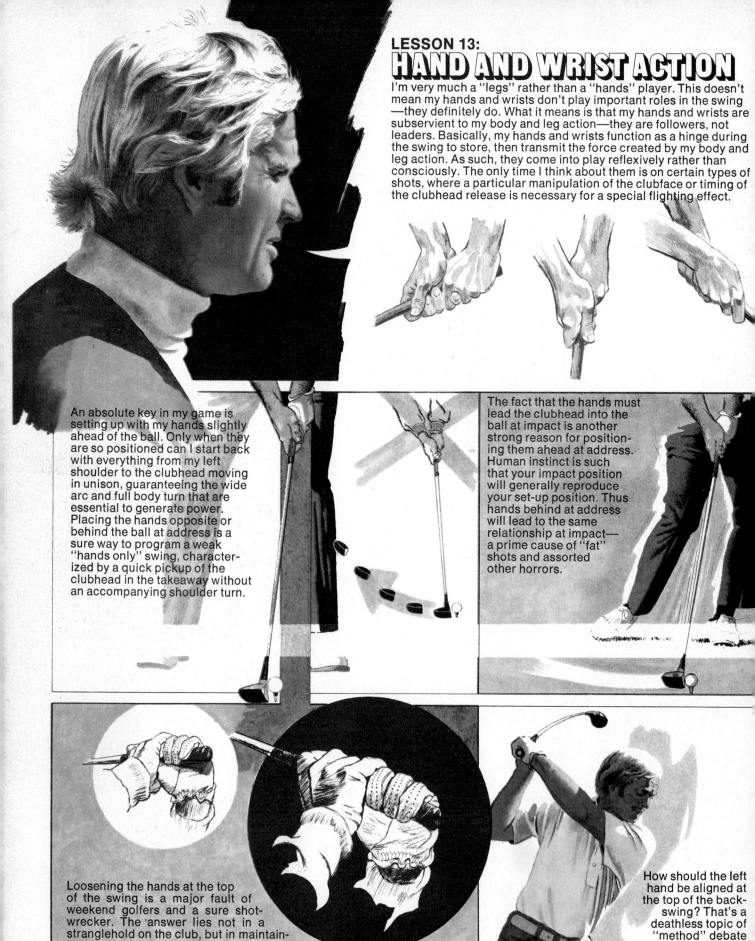

LESSON 13:
HAND AND WRIST ACTION

I'm very much a "legs" rather than a "hands" player. This doesn't mean my hands and wrists don't play important roles in the swing —they definitely do. What it means is that my hands and wrists are subservient to my body and leg action—they are followers, not leaders. Basically, my hands and wrists function as a hinge during the swing to store, then transmit the force created by my body and leg action. As such, they come into play reflexively rather than consciously. The only time I think about them is on certain types of shots, where a particular manipulation of the clubface or timing of the clubhead release is necessary for a special flighting effect.

An absolute key in my game is setting up with my hands slightly ahead of the ball. Only when they are so positioned can I start back with everything from my left shoulder to the clubhead moving in unison, guaranteeing the wide arc and full body turn that are essential to generate power. Placing the hands opposite or behind the ball at address is a sure way to program a weak "hands only" swing, characterized by a quick pickup of the clubhead in the takeaway without an accompanying shoulder turn.

The fact that the hands must lead the clubhead into the ball at impact is another strong reason for positioning them ahead at address. Human instinct is such that your impact position will generally reproduce your set-up position. Thus hands behind at address will lead to the same relationship at impact— a prime cause of "fat" shots and assorted other horrors.

Loosening the hands at the top of the swing is a major fault of weekend golfers and a sure shot-wrecker. The answer lies not in a stranglehold on the club, but in maintaining a consistent degree of firmness in the hands. Remember, however, that if you haven't got the club back adequately by turning your body, loosening your grip is going to be instinct's way of getting it there.

How should the left hand be aligned at the top of the back-swing? That's a deathless topic of "method" debate that really is unanswerable— it depends on the individual.

Superbly coordinated hands have been responsible for some great golf, but unskilled hands dominating the swing is a prime cause of high handicaps. The main problem is a tendency of the hands to operate independently of the rest of the body. This is most evident among 90-plus shooters at the start of the swing—a fast, jerking back of the clubhead by the hands inhibits correct body coiling.

My hands perform one almost imperceptible but, to me, very vital movement even before they play any role in the actual swing. This is a pressing-together action on the club-shaft just before I start the club back. It serves three purposes—it establishes my correct grip pressure, it tells all the muscles in my body that it's time for work and it serves as a motion from which I can fluently but deliberately swing the club back in a coordinated one-piece motion of hands, wrists, arms and shoulders.

I make no effort either to cock or keep from cocking my wrists on the backswing. What I do is simply try to maintain my original start-back grip pressure, thus allowing the swinging weight of the clubhead to cock my wrists naturally as my arms reach out and up. Photographs show that this cocking is a gradual process, beginning as the clubhead passes hip height and continuing smoothly into the start of the downswing.

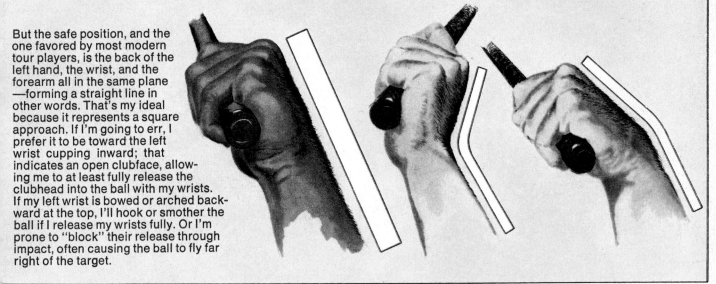

But the safe position, and the one favored by most modern tour players, is the back of the left hand, the wrist, and the forearm all in the same plane —forming a straight line in other words. That's my ideal because it represents a square approach. If I'm going to err, I prefer it to be toward the left wrist cupping inward; that indicates an open clubface, allowing me to at least fully release the clubhead into the ball with my wrists. If my left wrist is bowed or arched backward at the top, I'll hook or smother the ball if I release my wrists fully. Or I'm prone to "block" their release through impact, often causing the ball to fly far right of the target.

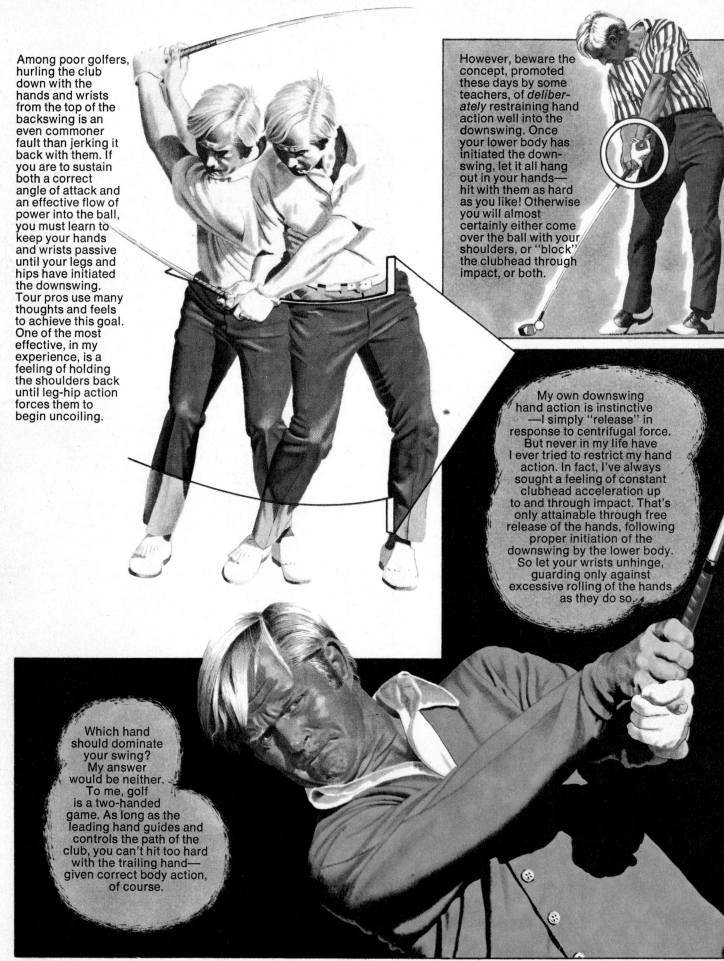

Among poor golfers, hurling the club down with the hands and wrists from the top of the backswing is an even commoner fault than jerking it back with them. If you are to sustain both a correct angle of attack and an effective flow of power into the ball, you must learn to keep your hands and wrists passive until your legs and hips have initiated the downswing. Tour pros use many thoughts and feels to achieve this goal. One of the most effective, in my experience, is a feeling of holding the shoulders back until leg-hip action forces them to begin uncoiling.

However, beware the concept, promoted these days by some teachers, of *deliberately* restraining hand action well into the downswing. Once your lower body has initiated the downswing, let it all hang out in your hands—hit with them as hard as you like! Otherwise you will almost certainly either come over the ball with your shoulders, or "block" the clubhead through impact, or both.

My own downswing hand action is instinctive—I simply "release" in response to centrifugal force. But never in my life have I ever tried to restrict my hand action. In fact, I've always sought a feeling of constant clubhead acceleration up to and through impact. That's only attainable through free release of the hands, following proper initiation of the downswing by the lower body. So let your wrists unhinge, guarding only against excessive rolling of the hands as they do so.

Which hand should dominate your swing? My answer would be neither. To me, golf is a two-handed game. As long as the leading hand guides and controls the path of the club, you can't hit too hard with the trailing hand—given correct body action, of course.

LESSON 14:
TIMING

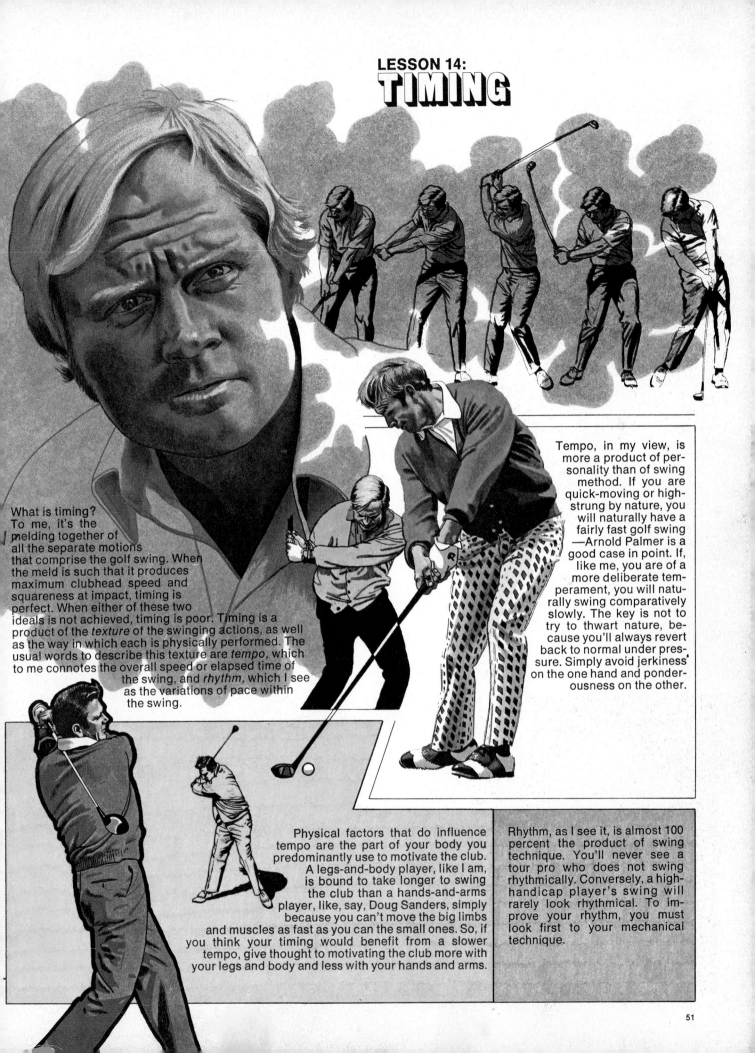

What is timing? To me, it's the melding together of all the separate motions that comprise the golf swing. When the meld is such that it produces maximum clubhead speed and squareness at impact, timing is perfect. When either of these two ideals is not achieved, timing is poor. Timing is a product of the *texture* of the swinging actions, as well as the way in which each is physically performed. The usual words to describe this texture are *tempo,* which to me connotes the overall speed or elapsed time of the swing, and *rhythm,* which I see as the variations of pace within the swing.

Tempo, in my view, is more a product of personality than of swing method. If you are quick-moving or high-strung by nature, you will naturally have a fairly fast golf swing —Arnold Palmer is a good case in point. If, like me, you are of a more deliberate temperament, you will naturally swing comparatively slowly. The key is not to try to thwart nature, because you'll always revert back to normal under pressure. Simply avoid jerkiness on the one hand and ponderousness on the other.

Physical factors that do influence tempo are the part of your body you predominantly use to motivate the club. A legs-and-body player, like I am, is bound to take longer to swing the club than a hands-and-arms player, like, say, Doug Sanders, simply because you can't move the big limbs and muscles as fast as you can the small ones. So, if you think your timing would benefit from a slower tempo, give thought to motivating the club more with your legs and body and less with your hands and arms.

Rhythm, as I see it, is almost 100 percent the product of swing technique. You'll never see a tour pro who does not swing rhythmically. Conversely, a high-handicap player's swing will rarely look rhythmical. To improve your rhythm, you must look first to your mechanical technique.

Throughout my career I've found that I swing most rhythmically when I consciously try to keep the tempo of the downswing identical to that of the backswing. My key thought in so doing is usually, "Swing your hands and arms at the same pace coming down as you did going up—especially as you start the downswing." The hands and the arms inevitably will travel faster coming down than they did going back, but thinking of them not doing so—without any effort to actually check them, mind you—has always helped me.

Anytime your hands and wrists dominate your swing, you endanger tempo and rhythm. The reason lies in the fact that, because they are so used to moving quickly and independently of the rest of the body in everyday life, your hands will snatch the club back and forth ahead of the rest of your anatomy, given the slightest chance. This doesn't mean that the hands mustn't be used in the swing, but rather that they must be *synchronized* with all other body actions in order to properly time the delivery of the clubhead to the ball.

Losing your balance is a certain way to disrupt your rhythm, and thus your timing. Staying in balance during a full swing involves a lot of factors, but chief among them in my book are: (1) swinging from the *insides* of the feet; (2) swinging around a fixed upper-axis—in my case the back of the neck; (3) maintaining a consistently firm grip on the club throughout the swing.

"Grabbing" the club in the hands at some point in the swing—an extremely common fault born largely of anxiety—is a sure rhythm-wrecker. The way to prevent it is to hold the club lightly as you finalize your address, firm up your hands as the club starts back, then consciously try to maintain the same grip pressure from there on in. What will actually happen is that your hands will reflexively tighten on the club the nearer you get to impact. But this is a natural and spontaneous occurrence, not something that you have to consciously make happen.

Failing to go fully back before you start down is a certain way to destroy rhythm, because it provokes a hurried transition of motion as the swing changes directions. "Complete your backswing" is one of my most frequent self-instructions, especially under pressure. The trick is to determine a definite set of feelings—related primarily to shoulder turn and hand height—that represent your full backswing, then allow yourself to realize them before you start down to the ball.

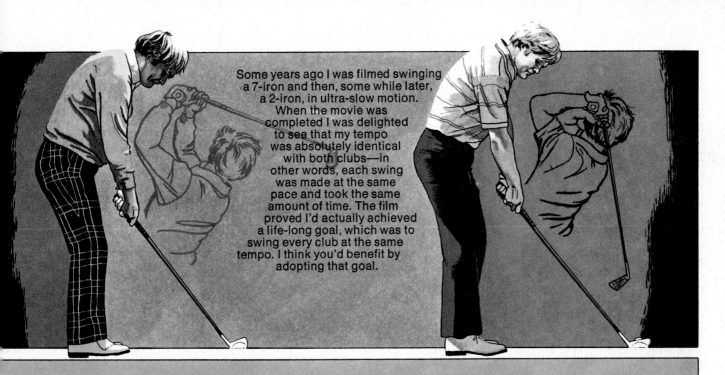

Some years ago I was filmed swinging a 7-iron and then, some while later, a 2-iron, in ultra-slow motion. When the movie was completed I was delighted to see that my tempo was absolutely identical with both clubs—in other words, each swing was made at the same pace and took the same amount of time. The film proved I'd actually achieved a life-long goal, which was to swing every club at the same tempo. I think you'd benefit by adopting that goal.

The most important single move in establishing your tempo and rhythm is your takeaway. It sets the beat for everything that comes later. For this reason, I strive on every shot to move the club back as *deliberately* as possible, consistent with swinging rather than "placing" or manipulating it.

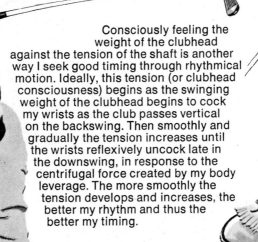

Consciously feeling the weight of the clubhead against the tension of the shaft is another way I seek good timing through rhythmical motion. Ideally, this tension (or clubhead consciousness) begins as the swinging weight of the clubhead begins to cock my wrists as the club passes vertical on the backswing. Then smoothly and gradually the tension increases until the wrists reflexively uncock late in the downswing, in response to the centrifugal force created by my body leverage. The more smoothly the tension develops and increases, the better my rhythm and thus the better my timing.

53

PART 3: CURES FOR COMMON PROBLEMS

LESSON 15:
HOOKING AND DRAWING

The drawn ball is to golf what the home run is to baseball —the strongest shot in the game, but the toughest to accomplish. It is achieved by imparting slight counterclockwise sidespin to the ball, hitting it with the clubhead traveling slightly from in to out across the target line and the clubface slightly closed to that swing path (pointing left of it). The draw becomes a hook when "slight" becomes acute in both cases.

I generally draw the ball only when a situation requires a right-to-left shot. One reason I've rarely used a draw as my basic "shape" is that it can easily degenerate into a hook. After the shank, this is the most destructive shot in golf. However, because of the strong swing pattern the draw demands, and the extra distance it produces, the less powerful golfer is generally better off cultivating a draw than a fade, even at the risk of the occasional hook.

It is almost a reflex move, when your ball continually finishes way left, to aim yourself more and more right at address. As we also saw last month, this affects the direction of the swing, in that the clubhead path at impact tends to match the alignment of the shoulders, which tend at impact to mirror their positions at address. Therein lies the source of your acutely in-to-out clubhead path.

To match your swing path to your target line, adjust your setup until your shoulders are parallel to that line at address. And remember that it is easier to set up square in the shoulders when you also set your feet and hips square to the target line.

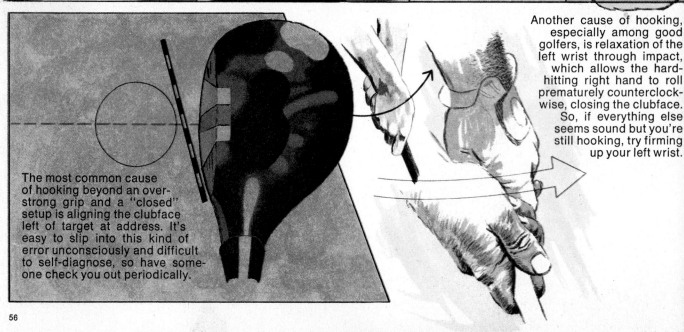

The most common cause of hooking beyond an over-strong grip and a "closed" setup is aligning the clubface left of target at address. It's easy to slip into this kind of error unconsciously and difficult to self-diagnose, so have someone check you out periodically.

Another cause of hooking, especially among good golfers, is relaxation of the left wrist through impact, which allows the hard-hitting right hand to roll prematurely counterclockwise, closing the clubface. So, if everything else seems sound but you're still hooking, try firming up your left wrist.

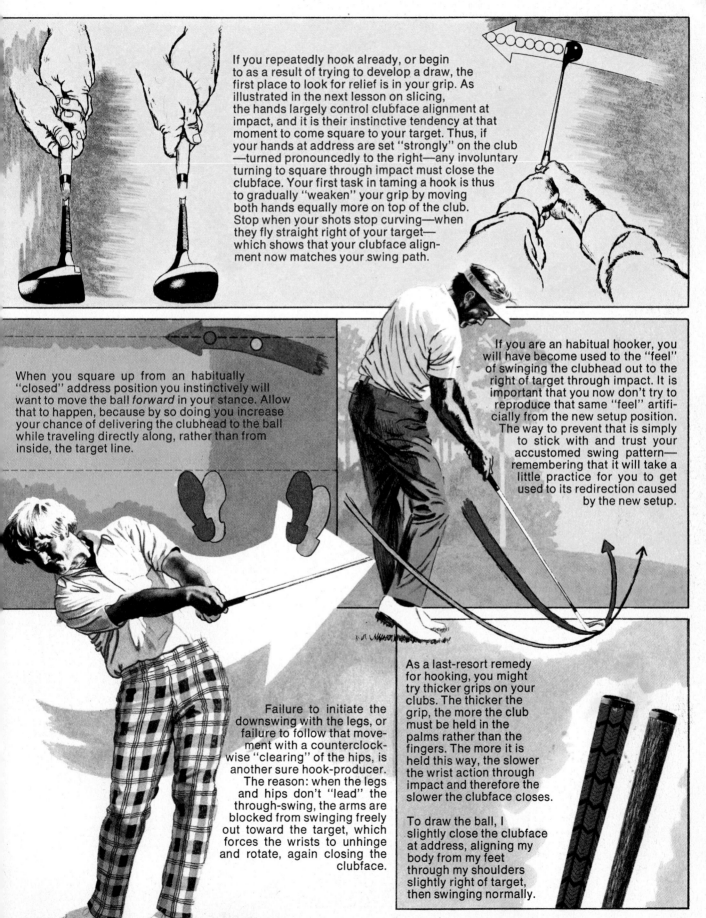

If you repeatedly hook already, or begin to as a result of trying to develop a draw, the first place to look for relief is in your grip. As illustrated in the next lesson on slicing, the hands largely control clubface alignment at impact, and it is their instinctive tendency at that moment to come square to your target. Thus, if your hands at address are set "strongly" on the club —turned pronouncedly to the right—any involuntary turning to square through impact must close the clubface. Your first task in taming a hook is thus to gradually "weaken" your grip by moving both hands equally more on top of the club. Stop when your shots stop curving—when they fly straight right of your target— which shows that your clubface alignment now matches your swing path.

When you square up from an habitually "closed" address position you instinctively will want to move the ball *forward* in your stance. Allow that to happen, because by so doing you increase your chance of delivering the clubhead to the ball while traveling directly along, rather than from inside, the target line.

If you are an habitual hooker, you will have become used to the "feel" of swinging the clubhead out to the right of target through impact. It is important that you now don't try to reproduce that same "feel" artificially from the new setup position. The way to prevent that is simply to stick with and trust your accustomed swing pattern— remembering that it will take a little practice for you to get used to its redirection caused by the new setup.

Failure to initiate the downswing with the legs, or failure to follow that movement with a counterclockwise "clearing" of the hips, is another sure hook-producer. The reason: when the legs and hips don't "lead" the through-swing, the arms are blocked from swinging freely out toward the target, which forces the wrists to unhinge and rotate, again closing the clubface.

As a last-resort remedy for hooking, you might try thicker grips on your clubs. The thicker the grip, the more the club must be held in the palms rather than the fingers. The more it is held this way, the slower the wrist action through impact and therefore the slower the clubface closes.

To draw the ball, I slightly close the clubface at address, aligning my body from my feet through my shoulders slightly right of target, then swinging normally.

A fade, or in other words a very small slice, has been my bread-and-butter shot throughout most of my career. Here's how I set up for it. Note that I will swing back *not* on the *actual* target line, but on the line *parallel* to my *body alignment,* which is slightly "open." This puts the club on a slightly out-to-in path relative to the target line. It also means that the clubface—although it is square to the actual target—is slightly open to my swing path. The result is that the club spins the ball a little left to right by cutting across it slightly at impact.

LESSON 16:
SLICING

Slicing is to golf like the common cold is to medicine —epidemic and seemingly incurable. It has dozens of causes, but *basically* it occurs because the golfer imparts left-to-right sidespin to the ball by hitting it with the clubhead traveling from out to in across the target line and the clubface open—pointing to the right of the swing path.

I've used a small slice—a fade—as my bread-and-butter shot throughout most of my amateur and professional career. But there's a big difference between this shot and the 90-plus-shooter's standard curve ball. My objective is to start the ball very slightly left of target and allow it to drift gently back on line as it nears the end of its flight. The hacker's habitual pattern is a shot that generally starts well left of target, then curves violently right soon after it leaves the clubface. It's the weakest shot in golf in terms of both distance and direction and is the main reason for high handicaps all over the world.

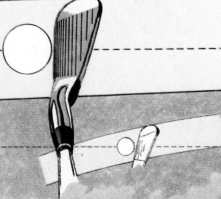

If slicing is your problem, understand first that the basic difference between your shot and mine is simply a matter of angles. In my fade, the clubhead is traveling only *very slightly* from outside the target line, and the clubhead is only *very slightly* open to that clubhead path at impact. In yours, the clubhead is arriving at the ball from well outside the target line with its face acutely open to that angle of delivery. Reduce those angles and your uncontrollable slice will turn into, at worst, a manageable fade.

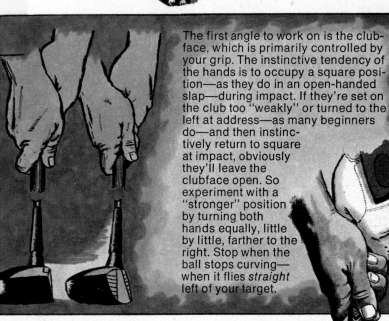

The first angle to work on is the club-face, which is primarily controlled by your grip. The instinctive tendency of the hands is to occupy a square position—as they do in an open-handed slap—during impact. If they're set on the club too "weakly" or turned too to the left at address—as many beginners do—and then instinctively return to square at impact, obviously they'll leave the clubface open. So experiment with a "stronger" position by turning both hands equally, little by little, farther to the right. Stop when the ball stops curving— when it flies *straight* left of your target.

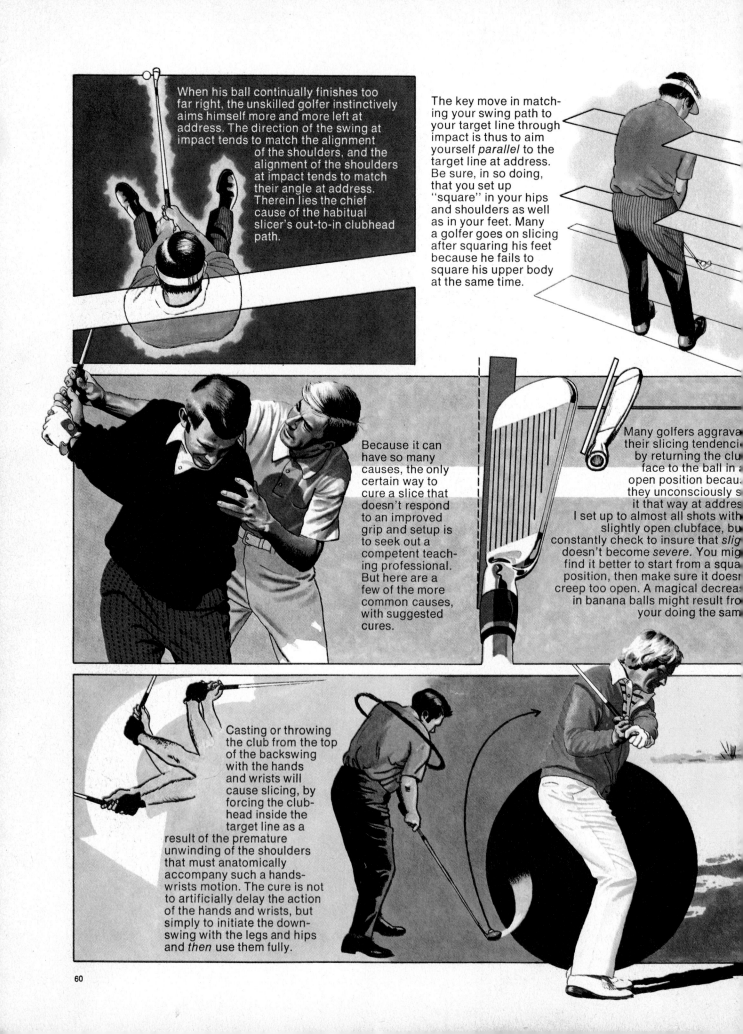

When his ball continually finishes too far right, the unskilled golfer instinctively aims himself more and more left at address. The direction of the swing at impact tends to match the alignment of the shoulders, and the alignment of the shoulders at impact tends to match their angle at address. Therein lies the chief cause of the habitual slicer's out-to-in clubhead path.

The key move in matching your swing path to your target line through impact is thus to aim yourself *parallel* to the target line at address. Be sure, in so doing, that you set up "square" in your hips and shoulders as well as in your feet. Many a golfer goes on slicing after squaring his feet because he fails to square his upper body at the same time.

Because it can have so many causes, the only certain way to cure a slice that doesn't respond to an improved grip and setup is to seek out a competent teaching professional. But here are a few of the more common causes, with suggested cures.

Many golfers aggrava their slicing tendenci by returning the clu face to the ball in open position becau they unconsciously s it that way at addres I set up to almost all shots with slightly open clubface, bu constantly check to insure that *slig* doesn't become *severe.* You mig find it better to start from a squa position, then make sure it doesn creep too open. A magical decrea in banana balls might result fro your doing the sam

Casting or throwing the club from the top of the backswing with the hands and wrists will cause slicing, by forcing the club-head inside the target line as a result of the premature unwinding of the shoulders that must anatomically accompany such a hands-wrists motion. The cure is not to artificially delay the action of the hands and wrists, but simply to initiate the downswing with the legs and hips and *then* use them fully.

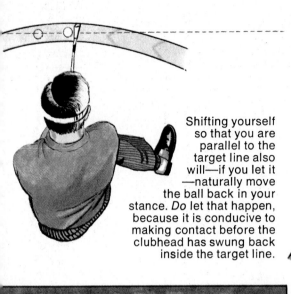

Shifting yourself so that you are parallel to the target line also will—if you let it —naturally move the ball back in your stance. *Do* let that happen, because it is conducive to making contact before the clubhead has swung back inside the target line.

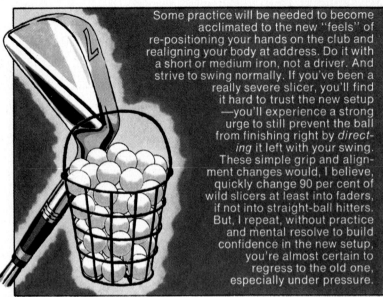

Some practice will be needed to become acclimated to the new "feels" of re-positioning your hands on the club and realigning your body at address. Do it with a short or medium iron, not a driver. And strive to swing normally. If you've been a really severe slicer, you'll find it hard to trust the new setup —you'll experience a strong urge to still prevent the ball from finishing right by *directing* it left with your swing. These simple grip and alignment changes would, I believe, quickly change 90 per cent of wild slicers at least into faders, if not into straight-ball hitters. But, I repeat, without practice and mental resolve to build confidence in the new setup, you're almost certain to regress to the old one, especially under pressure.

A prime cause of slicing among all golfers is a subconscious or involuntary tightening of the grip at some point during the swing. The right hand is generally the biggest culprit, grabbing the club so tightly that the wrists cannot release freely and fully through impact. The result is at least an open clubface. At worst, there is both an open clubface and an out-to-in swing path as a result of the right shoulder being pulled forward by the rigid wrists. The cure lies in maintaining an evenly firm grip pressure throughout the swing.

Spinning the entire body to the left early in the downswing provokes slicing, in that it also forces the club forward and thus across the target line before impact. The cure, again, is to lead with the legs— shuttling both knees smoothly targetward before the shoulders uncoil or the hands/wrists release.

J McQueen

TOPPING AND FAT SHOTS

Topping is hitting the ball anywhere above its equator. The first thing you must understand in order to prevent this is that you can actually do it in two distinctly different ways. Probably the most common cause of topping among regular golfers is swinging down so steeply into the ball that the clubhead does not get low enough to contact the back of the ball before it has passed *beyond* the ball. Chronic slicers and pullers generally top shots this way, although it can happen occasionally even to the good player, especially when hitting "late" with the hands in trying to drive the ball low.

The cure again is radical improvement of the overall swing pattern, but keeping the weight predominantly on the left side throughout the swing sometimes helps a beginner temporarily. The more experienced player should practice leading the downswing with the legs and hips, rather than the hands and wrists.

Occasionally on tour you'll see a golfer (including myself) "cold top" a driver or a long iron. In fact, it's the most common way in which really skilled golfers flat miss the ball. The cause here is almost always trying to "kill" the shot, which generates an acceleration of the leg and hip action that in turn overdelays the release of the clubhead into the ball by the hands and wrists.

Hitting fat is hitting the ground before the ball. A lot of golfers do it all the time without ever recognizing the fact, which is one reason their shots lack both distance and the bite on landing that comes from backspin.

All the factors that I mentioned as causing topping can also cause fat hitting, depending simply on whether or not the clubhead touches the ground before it reaches the ball. Thus the *basic* cure for hitting fat is exactly the same as for topping—a radical improvement in over-all swing pattern.

If you don't want to go to that trouble, then at least look to your leg action. Almost any time a golfer on tour hits a noticeably fat shot, it's because he has delivered the clubhead with his hands and wrists fractionally ahead of his leg and hip action. Most amateurs do this all their lives, and would be delightfully surprised at the purer shots they would hit simply by learning how to *lead* the clubhead *through* the ball with an uncoiling action of their legs and hips.

The only sure way to overcome this kind of topping is to widen your downswing arc so that the clubhead can meet the back of the ball traveling at ground level. The only certain way to do that is to improve your over-all swing pattern. However, a temporary "Band-Aid" cure can sometimes be effected simply by moving the ball and your head back at address, then concentrating on keeping your head back through impact.

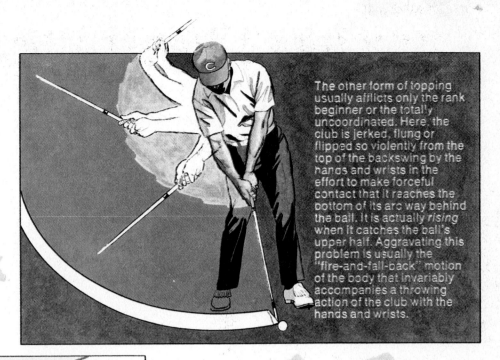

The other form of topping usually afflicts only the rank beginner or the totally uncoordinated. Here, the club is jerked, flung or flipped so violently from the top of the backswing by the hands and wrists in the effort to make forceful contact that it reaches the bottom of its arc way behind the ball. It is actually *rising* when it catches the ball's upper half. Aggravating this problem is usually the "fire-and-fall-back" motion of the body that invariably accompanies a throwing action of the club with the hands and wrists.

One other cause of topping that afflicts both skilled and indifferent golfers at times is swaying. Any lateral movement—as opposed to a coiling movement—of the body on the backswing moves the swing arc backward. Obviously, if it isn't then moved forward a similar amount during the downswing, the low point of the club's arc is going to be behind the ball, causing at best a "thin" shot and at worst a topped or "fat" shot. The simple way to overcome this is to keep your head in the same place throughout the swing. It's impossible to sway if your head doesn't move.

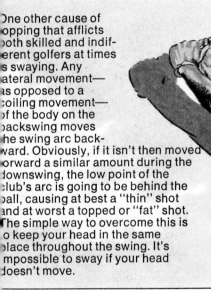

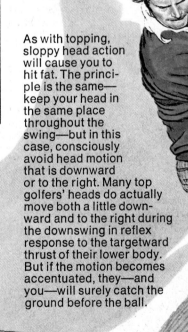

As with topping, sloppy head action will cause you to hit fat. The principle is the same— keep your head in the same place throughout the swing—but in this case, consciously avoid head motion that is downward or to the right. Many top golfers' heads do actually move both a little downward and to the right during the downswing in reflex response to the targetward thrust of their lower body. But if the motion becomes accentuated, they—and you—will surely catch the ground before the ball.

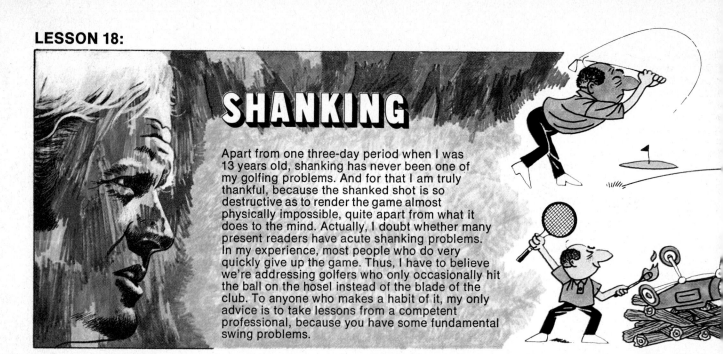

SHANKING

Apart from one three-day period when I was 13 years old, shanking has never been one of my golfing problems. And for that I am truly thankful, because the shanked shot is so destructive as to render the game almost physically impossible, quite apart from what it does to the mind. Actually, I doubt whether many present readers have acute shanking problems. In my experience, most people who do very quickly give up the game. Thus, I have to believe we're addressing golfers who only occasionally hit the ball on the hosel instead of the blade of the club. To anyone who makes a habit of it, my only advice is to take lessons from a competent professional, because you have some fundamental swing problems.

Even when a golfer sets up effectively at address, an acute casting or throwing of the club with the hands and wrists from the top of the backswing will move the club so far outward that its hosel rather than its blade contacts the ball. Beginning the downswing with a counter-clockwise turn of the shoulders can have the same effect—especially when combined with a casting motion of the hands and wrists. The antidote in both cases is to be passive in the upper body while initiating the downswing with the feet, legs and hips.

A pro-am partner of mine some years back suffered from a dreadful shank, besides hitting every wood shot off of the heel (they go together). We cured him instantly by simply getting him to set his weight back more toward his heels at address and stay there throughout the swing. He'd been almost up on his tippy-toes at address, which caused him to fall forward on every shot.

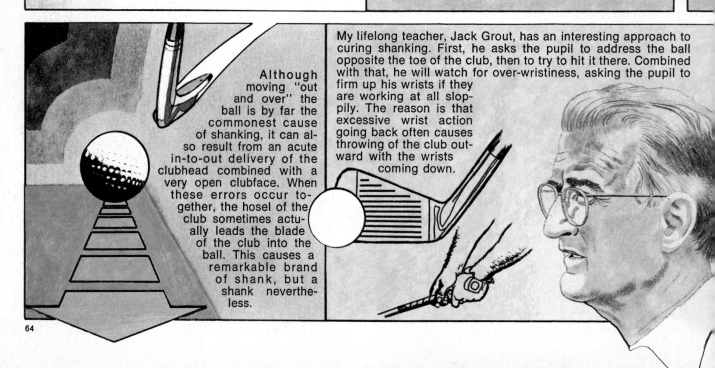

Although moving "out and over" the ball is by far the commonest cause of shanking, it can also result from an acute in-to-out delivery of the clubhead combined with a very open clubface. When these errors occur together, the hosel of the club sometimes actually leads the blade of the club into the ball. This causes a remarkable brand of shank, but a shank nevertheless.

My lifelong teacher, Jack Grout, has an interesting approach to curing shanking. First, he asks the pupil to address the ball opposite the toe of the club, then to try to hit it there. Combined with that, he will watch for over-wristiness, asking the pupil to firm up his wrists if they are working at all sloppily. The reason is that excessive wrist action going back often causes throwing of the club outward with the wrists coming down.

The basic cause of shanking is simply a movement *outward* of the club at some point in the swing prior to impact. To put it another way, the golfer (assuming he addresses the ball correctly opposite the center of the clubface) somehow shifts the entire plane of the club's path a couple of inches *farther* away from himself at some point in the swing. Let's look at the most common of those "somehows."

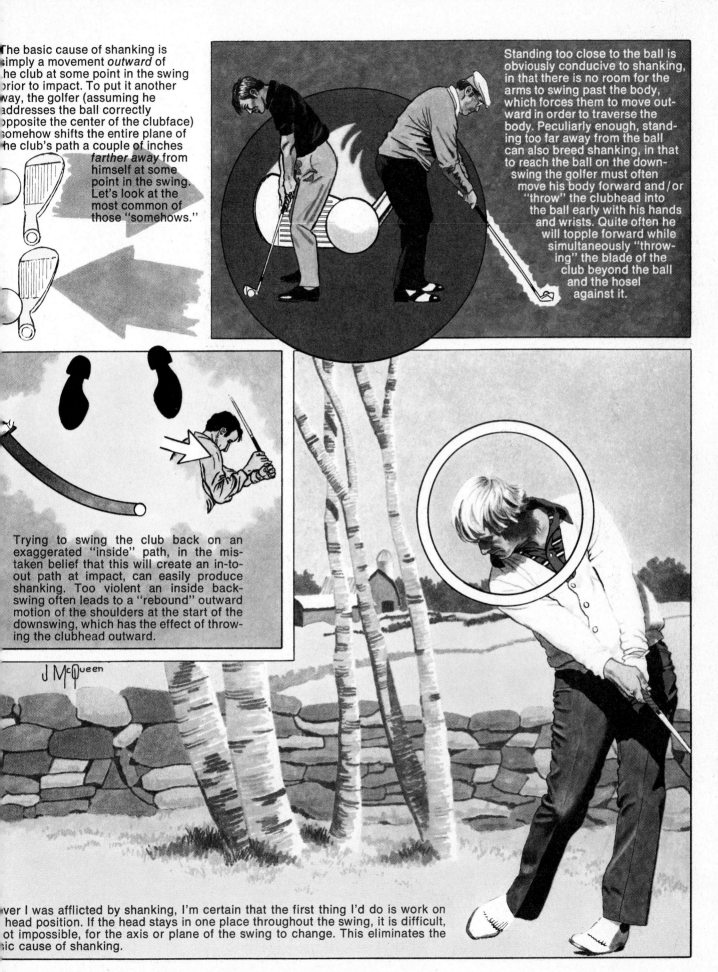

Standing too close to the ball is obviously conducive to shanking, in that there is no room for the arms to swing past the body, which forces them to move outward in order to traverse the body. Peculiarly enough, standing too far away from the ball can also breed shanking, in that to reach the ball on the downswing the golfer must often move his body forward and/or "throw" the clubhead into the ball early with his hands and wrists. Quite often he will topple forward while simultaneously "throwing" the blade of the club beyond the ball and the hosel against it.

Trying to swing the club back on an exaggerated "inside" path, in the mistaken belief that this will create an in-to-out path at impact, can easily produce shanking. Too violent an inside backswing often leads to a "rebound" outward motion of the shoulders at the start of the downswing, which has the effect of throwing the clubhead outward.

J McQueen

...ver I was afflicted by shanking, I'm certain that the first thing I'd do is work on ... head position. If the head stays in one place throughout the swing, it is difficult, ...ot impossible, for the axis or plane of the swing to change. This eliminates the ...sic cause of shanking.

PART 4: THE SHORT GAME

CHIPPING

Chipping's like putting—you can do it effectively a number of ways. I prefer to use my wrists almost entirely in chipping, rather than the firm-wristed arm swing that some tour players prefer. The reason is simply that I get more sense of feel, or touch, with a hand-and-wrist motion than with a stiff-arm movement. Thus, in my case, any body action is merely a result of my wrist action. The stroke is made almost entirely by hinging, but not rolling, the wrists, with my arms traveling only a very short distance.

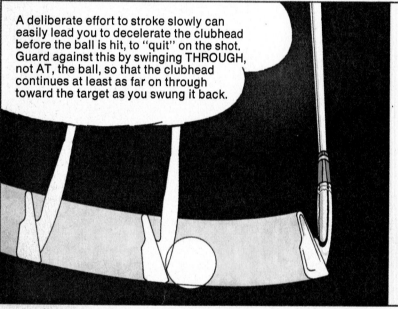

A deliberate effort to stroke slowly can easily lead you to decelerate the clubhead before the ball is hit, to "quit" on the shot. Guard against this by swinging THROUGH, not AT, the ball, so that the clubhead continues at least as far on through toward the target as you swung it back.

Remember that on the normal chip shot, to keep the clubface square to the target the right hand must go UNDER, not roll over, the left on the through-swing. The right hand releases against a firm, guiding left hand.

If you're a poor chipper, check where you hold the club. Choking down on the grip will increase your control and make it easier for you to strike the ball accurately and firmly. I see many club golfers chipping with a full-shot grip high on the club. I believe they'd improve if they kept their hands and the clubface closer together.

Another mistake club golfers make is to position the ball too far from their feet. This encourages swinging the clubhead across the target line. They'd probably get better results with a more straight-back-straight-through swing path, achieved by playing the ball closer in.

For example, I believe many pushed and pulled chips are most commonly caused by playing the ball too far from the feet. This positioning causes the golfer to reach for the ball, and also to unnecessarily manipulate the clubface. You'll also tend to push the ball if you play it back too far, opposite your right foot; the clubhead will still be moving on an inside-out path when it meets the ball.

To me, the most important aspect of the chipping stroke is its speed. I seek to make an easy-yet-firm swing, but above all a SLOW swing. It is so easy on these little shots to jab or jerk at the ball that I almost always have to make a conscious effort to stroke chip shots slowly. This is one of the hardest things I've had to learn in golf—and I'm still learning.

SLOW

I try to stand comfortably for a chip shot, with my feet close together, my body relaxed, and my eyes over the ball. As in putting, I regard a stationary head as an absolute prerequisite of success. My stance is slightly open to the left to allow my hands and arms to swing through to the target, and my weight remains predominantly on my left foot throughout the stroke. I make no weight transfer during the stroke—doing so would ruin the shot by increasing the clubhead's speed.

To chip effectively, your hands MUST be ahead of the clubface at impact. This relationship is most easily achieved by setting your hands forward of the ball at address. They can then lead the entire forward stroke, helping insure striking the ball before brushing the turf. The most fatal chipping mistake of club golfers is to try to scoop the ball up, instead of swinging the clubhead crisply FORWARD and DOWN into the ball.

When you practice chipping, concentrate on developing TECHNIQUE. Select a good lie and hit one kind of shot until you can produce the same action and result every time. Moving quickly from one type of chip to another of varying length may help improve your touch, but the first priority is to develop a sound basic chipping technique.

J McQueen

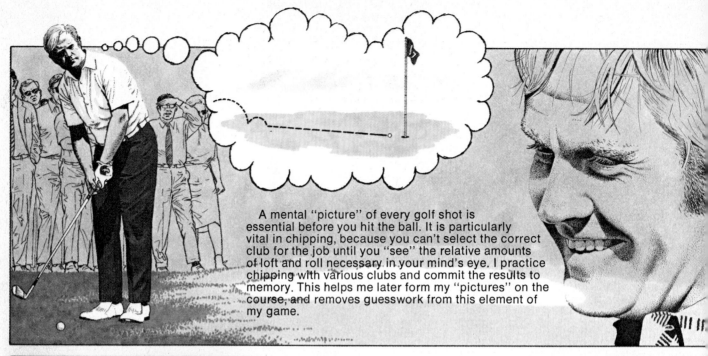

A mental "picture" of every golf shot is essential before you hit the ball. It is particularly vital in chipping, because you can't select the correct club for the job until you "see" the relative amounts of loft and roll necessary in your mind's eye. I practice chipping with various clubs and commit the results to memory. This helps me later form my "pictures" on the course, and removes guesswork from this element of my game.

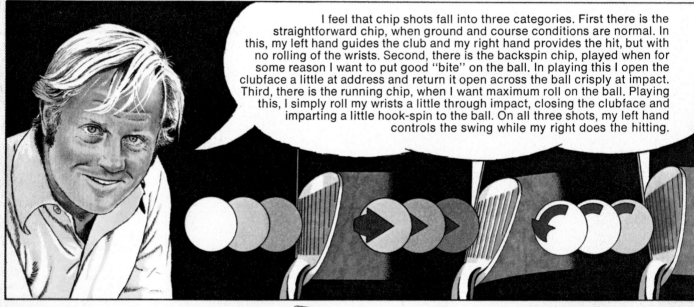

I feel that chip shots fall into three categories. First there is the straightforward chip, when ground and course conditions are normal. In this, my left hand guides the club and my right hand provides the hit, but with no rolling of the wrists. Second, there is the backspin chip, played when for some reason I want to put good "bite" on the ball. In playing this I open the clubface a little at address and return it open across the ball crisply at impact. Third, there is the running chip, when I want maximum roll on the ball. Playing this, I simply roll my wrists a little through impact, closing the clubface and imparting a little hook-spin to the ball. On all three shots, my left hand controls the swing while my right does the hitting.

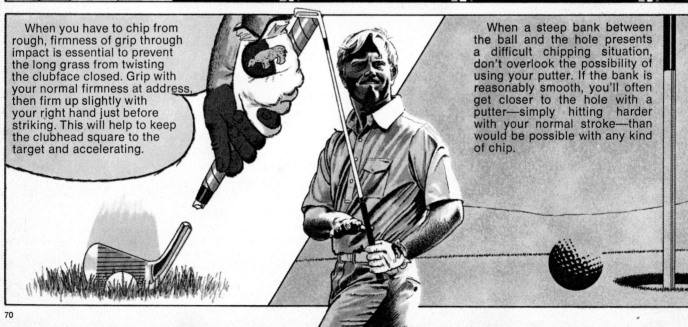

When you have to chip from rough, firmness of grip through impact is essential to prevent the long grass from twisting the clubface closed. Grip with your normal firmness at address, then firm up slightly with your right hand just before striking. This will help to keep the clubhead square to the target and accelerating.

When a steep bank between the ball and the hole presents a difficult chipping situation, don't overlook the possibility of using your putter. If the bank is reasonably smooth, you'll often get closer to the hole with a putter—simply hitting harder with your normal stroke—than would be possible with any kind of chip.

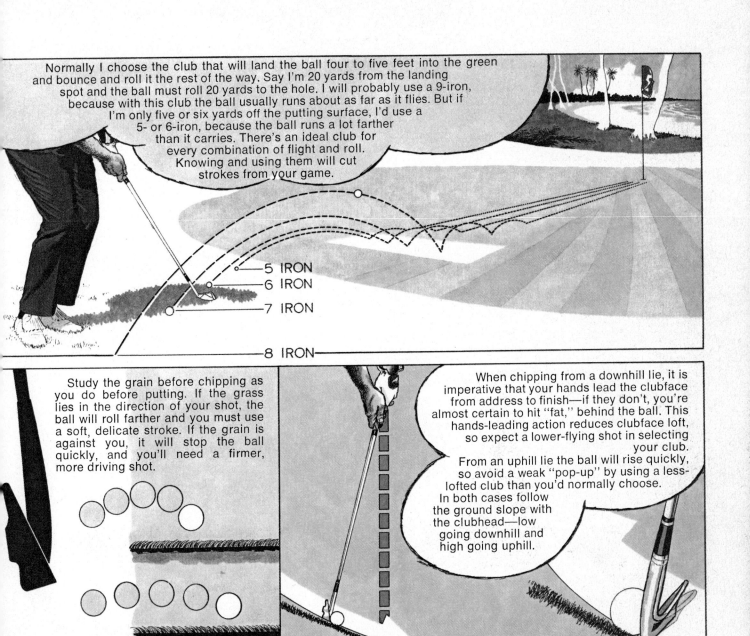

Normally I choose the club that will land the ball four to five feet into the green and bounce and roll it the rest of the way. Say I'm 20 yards from the landing spot and the ball must roll 20 yards to the hole. I will probably use a 9-iron, because with this club the ball usually runs about as far as it flies. But if I'm only five or six yards off the putting surface, I'd use a 5- or 6-iron, because the ball runs a lot farther than it carries. There's an ideal club for every combination of flight and roll. Knowing and using them will cut strokes from your game.

5 IRON
6 IRON
7 IRON

8 IRON

Study the grain before chipping as you do before putting. If the grass lies in the direction of your shot, the ball will roll farther and you must use a soft, delicate stroke. If the grain is against you, it will stop the ball quickly, and you'll need a firmer, more driving shot.

When chipping from a downhill lie, it is imperative that your hands lead the clubface from address to finish—if they don't, you're almost certain to hit "fat," behind the ball. This hands-leading action reduces clubface loft, so expect a lower-flying shot in selecting your club.
From an uphill lie the ball will rise quickly, so avoid a weak "pop-up" by using a less-lofted club than you'd normally choose. In both cases follow the ground slope with the clubhead—low going downhill and high going uphill.

If my ball is in a trap with little or no lip, and the pin is way back into the green, I'll often play a chip rather than a regular sand shot. Normally I use an 8- or 9-iron, play the ball off my right heel, choke down on the grip and hood the clubface slightly. Then, with a very steady head, I try to hit firmly down on the ball without taking sand until after impact.

J. McQueen

FAIRWAY WEDGE PLAY

The most common mistake in fairway wedge play is trying to hit shots too hard. This results in loss of rhythm and timing—a skied shot on one hole, a skulled shot on the next. When you take the wedge from your bag, remember that with this club the ball should be caressed, not assaulted. The key to good wedge play, for me, is to swing easily yet firmly. While I never want to force a wedge shot, I want to avoid sloppy swinging—a danger any time you use less than your normal power. Concentrate on swinging slowly and smoothly, with firm hand action through impact.

Many golfers hit wedge shots with the ball positioned back towards the right foot. This brings the club into the ball at a very steep angle and also reduces the effective loft of the clubface. It seems to me they might as well play an 8- or 9-iron, because they are defeating the purposes of using the wedge—providing height and stopping power. On a normal wedge shot I play the ball where I do with all my other clubs—opposite my left heel. This position insures that my clubhead will meet the ball near the bottom of the swing arc and give me the high trajectory.

I swing the wedge primarily with my arms, keeping body movement to a minimum for best possible balance and accurate contact with the ball. My arm-swing is a little more upright than usual, so that the club will impart maximum height and backspin to the ball.

On wedge shots from heavy rough, play the ball back a little towards your right foot to minimize the amount of grass that will intervene between the ball and the clubface. Then swing down steeply enough to take quite a bit of turf in front of the ball. Most important of all, try to make a full follow-through. You might not succeed, but the thought of doing so will help you swing smoothly rather than beat at the ball as if it were a snake.

Any thought of swinging easier leads many golfers to quit on the shot. You can overcome this, as I do, by using a bit more wrist action on wedge shots than you would, say, with the driver. Maintain a firm hold on the club, but don't hesitate to add some "punch" to the shot with your wrist-action through impact.

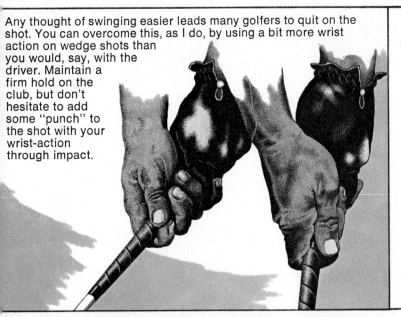

Stay firm on your feet with all wedge shots. At address set most of your weight on your left foot and keep most of it there throughout the swing. There'll automatically be a slight weight shift to the right on the backswing, but there's no need to lift or roll your left heel as you may do on fuller swings.

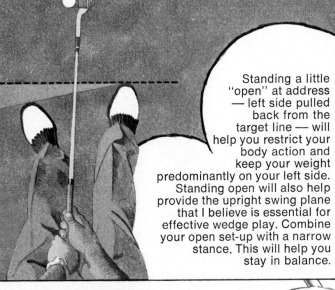

Standing a little "open" at address — left side pulled back from the target line — will help you restrict your body action and keep your weight predominantly on your left side. Standing open will also help provide the upright swing plane that I believe is essential for effective wedge play. Combine your open set-up with a narrow stance. This will help you stay in balance.

If your wedge swing is light and easy—as it should be —you may tend to collapse your arms through impact. While this doesn't happen so readily on the longer clubs and more forceful shots where sheer momentum helps to produce arm extension through the ball, I find that to hit crisp wedge shots I must make a conscious effort to EXTEND my arms through impact. I think of both arms straightening and the clubhead moving low and forward towards the target.

Course situations may demand that you play a variety of shots with the wedge, but I believe that on the practice tee you should work to perfect one kind of shot at a time. When you're playing the course, try to rely on the wedge shots you've mastered. If you find yourself needing another type, practice it thoroughly before you take it onto the course. The wedge is a great stroke-saver in skilled hands, but it can be a harmful stroke-waster if you lack experience with it.

LESSON 21:

PUTTING MECHANICS

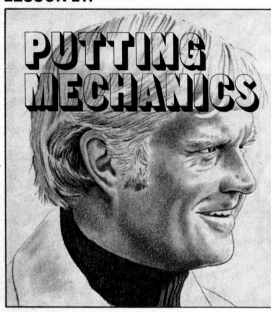

Most putting troubles stem from being scared or indecisive, or both. I find a positive attitude and procedure on the greens even more important than on the tee and from the fairway. I can often recover from a poor drive or approach, but a missed putt is a stroke gone forever.

The foundation of a positive putting attitude is a sound method of stroking the ball. If you lack confidence in **HOW** you're going to hit a putt you'll have even less about **WHERE** you're going to hit it.

I don't think it matters too much how a golfer arranges himself over his putts, so long as he meets two essentials. First, he must be solidly balanced, comfortable — an awkward stance inhibits smoothness of stroke. Second, the stance must allow the body and head to remain motionless.

Throughout my career, I have putted best with a feeling that I am set up **BEHIND** the ball, hitting it **AWAY** from me. Thus on all level putts I address the ball opposite my left toe and set my head well behind it.

Set up like this, I can look "through" the ball to my target. This particular optical angle is critical to my rolling the ball smoothly and squarely **FORWARD** along on the precise line I have chosen.

Looking **DIRECTLY DOWN** on the ball is vital for me, too. If my eyes are out beyond the ball, I tend to pull putts left; if my eyes are inside the line, I am prone to push putts right.

You can check your alignment by first assuming your usual head position over the ball, then taking one hand from the club and, with it, dropping another ball straight down from the bridge of your nose. To minimize movement, you might hold the test ball in your teeth until the transfer. Try this test for eye alignment if you regularly pull or push putts.

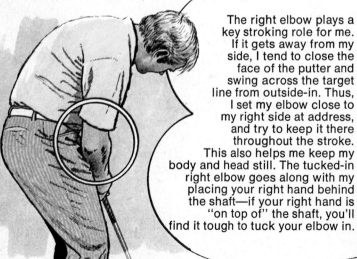

The right elbow plays a key stroking role for me. If it gets away from my side, I tend to close the face of the putter and swing across the target line from outside-in. Thus, I set my elbow close to my right side at address, and try to keep it there throughout the stroke. This also helps me keep my body and head still. The tucked-in right elbow goes along with my placing your right hand behind the shaft—if your right hand is "on top of" the shaft, you'll find it tough to tuck your elbow in.

Another focal stroking point for me is my left shoulder. My wife Barbara will often tell me after a poor putting round: "You're lifting your head again!" Actually, I'm not. What happens is that I unconsciously lift my left shoulder on the through swing, which causes my head to rise. Many poor putters do this without ever realizing it. Thinking of keeping the left shoulder "low" throughout the stroke might work wonders for them.

The hands are the critical factor in putting, because they totally control the alignment of the clubface, and almost totally the stroke itself.

On all putts, I have the feeling that my left hand guides the stroke and my right hand does the work, pushing the putterhead squarely through the ball. Thus I use and recommend the reverse overlap grip, which places all the fingers of the right hand on the club. I set my right hand **BEHIND** the shaft so that, if I opened my fingers, the palm would parallel the putterface. Most of the stroking force comes from my right forefinger—my "touch" finger—which is triggered around the grip.

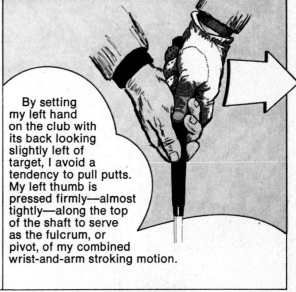

By setting my left hand on the club with its back looking slightly left of target, I avoid a tendency to pull putts. My left thumb is pressed firmly—almost tightly—along the top of the shaft to serve as the fulcrum, or pivot, of my combined wrist-and-arm stroking motion.

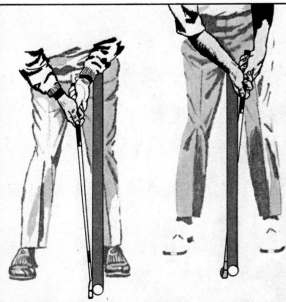

Another important angle, in my estimation, is the alignment of the putter-face at address and impact. Some players lay the shaft back with the hands behind the putterface at address, and return to this position at impact. This is an effective way to get the ball rolling—so long as you don't top it.

Other players angle the shaft forward with the hands ahead of the clubface at address and impact. This produces solid contact by virtue of a slightly downward blow, but, since the ball tends to be driven into the surface, it may react erratically on some greens.

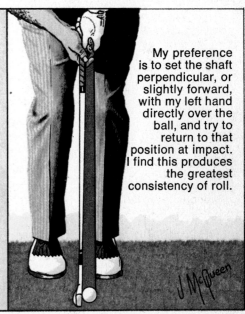

My preference is to set the shaft perpendicular, or slightly forward, with my left hand directly over the ball, and try to return to that position at impact. I find this produces the greatest consistency of roll.

J. McQueen

try to keep my actual stroke simple, ch to me means making a movement as ilar to a pendulum swing as possible.

THESE ARE MY KEY THOUGHTS:

tart the erhead ight back the ball, othly, ly, and URALLY.

2. Keep the putterhead low to the ground on the backswing and throughswing.

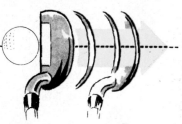

3. Swing firmly through the ball, ensuring that the putterhead does not decelerate before impact. Stroking at a constant speed back and through helps me to achieve this.

4. Keep the putterface square and moving along the initial direction line of putt for at least five inches after the ball is struck.

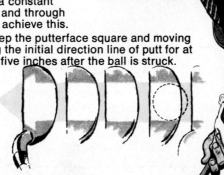

One final tip. I hold my breath during and just prior to making the stroke. By preventing the diaphragm from moving, this helps me to keep my body and head perfectly still.

The keys to good putting are a positive mental attitude and a basically sound stroke. First, analyze each shot from the green with as much care and precision as possible, then step up to the ball and execute the shot with confidence. Make sure that your backswing and throughswing follow along the target line at a smooth, constant tempo. The putterhead should be kept low to the ground on the backswing and throughswing. It should not decelerate before impact and it should be kept square and move along the initial direction line of the putt for at least five inches after the ball is struck.

LESSON 22:
PUTTING POINTERS

On the boundless subject of putting here are some pointers that have helped my game on the green over the years, and might clip a couple of strokes off yours.

In selecting a putter pay particular attention to how the club soles when you assume your most effective putting stance. You're going to have difficulty stroking the ball accurately with any putter that does not rest flat on the ground. If the heel sticks up, you need a more upright putter. If the toe is off the ground, you need a flatter-lying club. However, if the putter seems gorgeous in every other way, consider having your pro bend the shaft to produce your ideal angle of lie.

Should you putt stiff-wristed, using a shoulders-and-arms stroke like George Archer; with your hands and wrists more than the arms, like Bill Casper; or with a combined wrist-forearm action like Lee Trevino and me? The only way to answer that question is through experiment to discover which method works best for you. My experience runs the gamut. I putted stiff-wristed most of my amateur career, then went to an all-wrist stroke for better "touch" when I started encountering a wider variety of green conditions on turning pro. In recent years I've been basically a combined arms-and-wrists putter, and have become very comfortable with the naturalness of this technique.

My greens routine rarely varies. First, I determine the speed and direction of the putt. Next, I make a couple of practice swings, trying exactly to reproduce the stroke I'll apply to the ball. I then place the clubface behind the ball square to my selected line, and I position my feet and body to form a general stance. Finally, I make all the slight adjustments necessary for comfort and correct alignment as I glance at the lie of the putt by looking past my left shoulder.

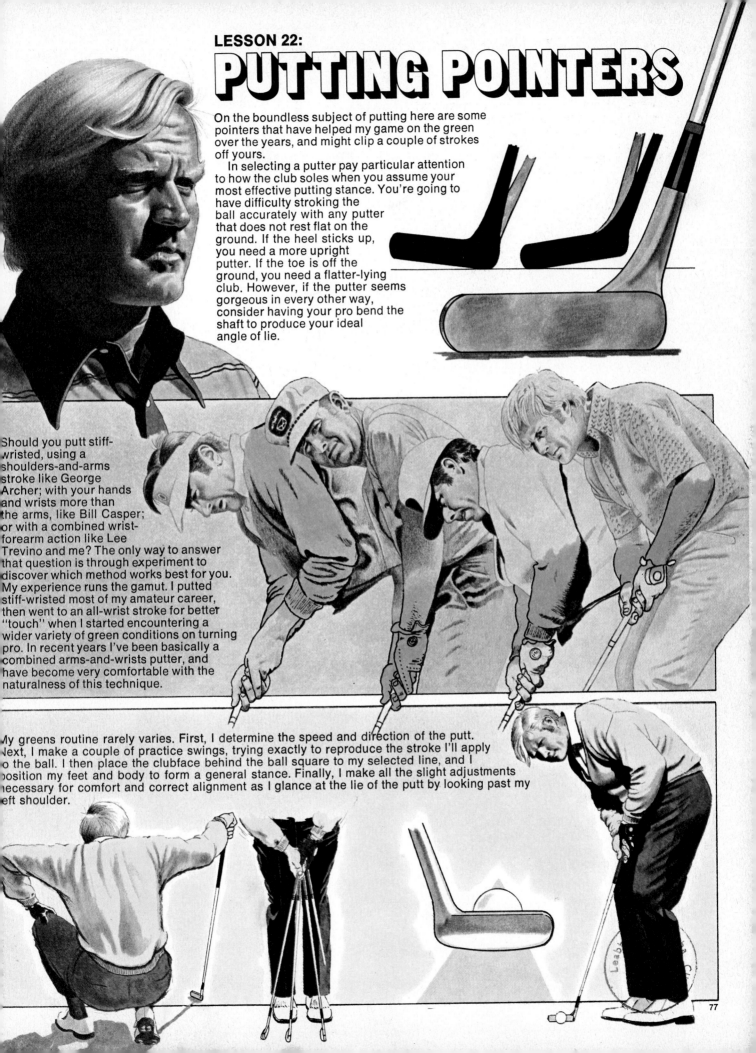

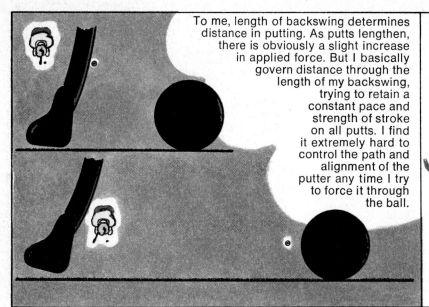

To me, length of backswing determines distance in putting. As putts lengthen, there is obviously a slight increase in applied force. But I basically govern distance through the length of my backswing, trying to retain a constant pace and strength of stroke on all putts. I find it extremely hard to control the path and alignment of the putter any time I try to force it through the ball.

I seek fluidity of clubhead movement in putting, and an important factor in achieving it is the firmness of my grip. I strive to hold the club firmly enough so that I can control its path and face alignment, but not so tightly that it cannot swing naturally of its own weight. Incidentally, I try to use the same grip pressure on all lengths and types of putts.

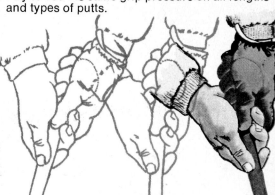

If you have trouble swinging the putter away from the ball smoothly, try going into your backswing off a slight forward press. Simply ease your wrists slightly towards the hole and then recoil into your backswing from this movement. Keep the action gentle—if you overdo it, you'll open the face of the putter.

Here's a wrinkle that's helped me from time to time. If I'm having difficulty stroking *through* the ball, I find that pointing my left elbow more to the hole helps me follow through by encouraging my left hand to keep moving through the ball. Conversely, if I'm having trouble striking the ball solidly, holding the left elbow close in against my side helps me deliver a firmer tap with my right hand.

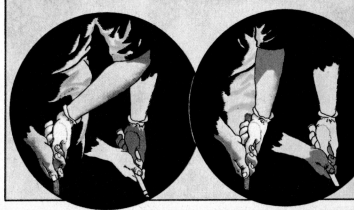

The better you learn to "read" greens, the better you'll putt. A subtle case in point concerns the two basic types of wet greens. When moisture has really soaked through the grass into the ground, a putt generally will run slower and break less than normal. It thus invites a firm, bold stroke. When greens are only filmed with moisture, as after a brief shower, generally they will play only very slightly slower than normal. So stroke delicately under these circumstances.

Do you ever get confused about the break of a putt when viewed from opposite sides of the hole? The solution usually lies in the surrounding terrain. It is more common for a putt to break with the general slope of the land. That's one reason I size up the scenery as I walk onto the greens at hilly courses.

The ideal way to distribute your weight in setting up to putt is to assume a stance that lets you feel comfortable while keeping your head and body motionless throughout the stroke. I generally best achieve both these objectives when I feel that my left heel is carrying slightly more of my weight. "Anchoring" myself on my left heel also reinforces my feeling of stability over the ball.

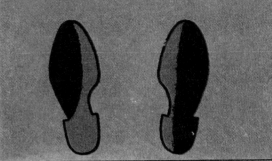

I find that any form of head or body movement during the stroke keeps me from contacting the ball solidly with the putter blade. Sometimes simply willing myself to "stay still" doesn't get the job done. When I find I am moving, I've often licked the problem just by making a deliberate effort to set my weight on the insides of my feet, still slightly toward the left heel. Anchored this way, I believe you'll find it equally hard to sway.

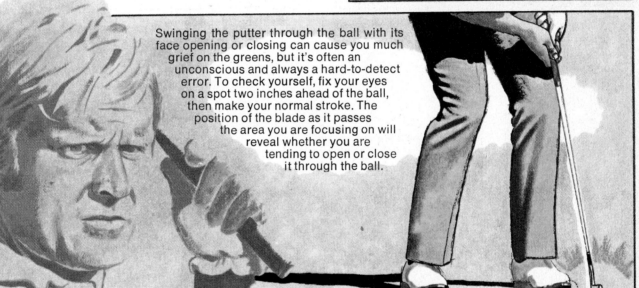

Swinging the putter through the ball with its face opening or closing can cause you much grief on the greens, but it's often an unconscious and always a hard-to-detect error. To check yourself, fix your eyes on a spot two inches ahead of the ball, then make your normal stroke. The position of the blade as it passes the area you are focusing on will reveal whether you are tending to open or close it through the ball.

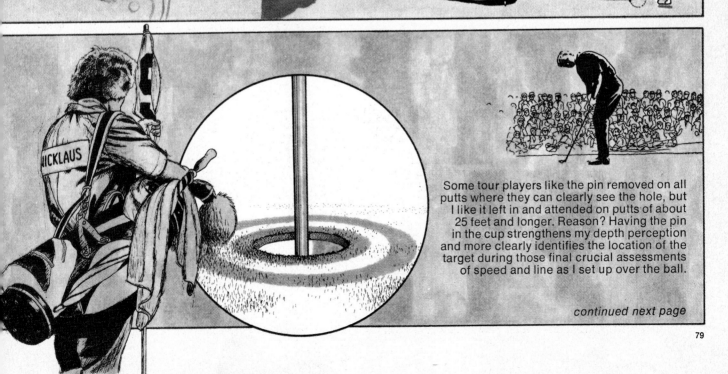

Some tour players like the pin removed on all putts where they can clearly see the hole, but I like it left in and attended on putts of about 25 feet and longer. Reason? Having the pin in the cup strengthens my depth perception and more clearly identifies the location of the target during those final crucial assessments of speed and line as I set up over the ball.

continued next page

If your game is being destroyed by three-putt greens, give some consideration to your approach club selection as well as to your putting stroke. Playing the Pleasant Valley course in Worcester, Mass., (currently site of the Pleasant Valley Classic), I discovered that the second green is 78 yards long and that the 14th green was a 4-iron to the front and a 3-wood to the back! Poor club selection on this kind of layout is bound to result in a bad case of the three-putts. Incidentally, on a strange course, you can learn a lot about green sizes and approach shot distances by relating to the size of the figures in the foursome ahead of you.

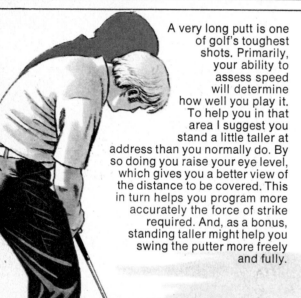

A very long putt is one of golf's toughest shots. Primarily, your ability to assess speed will determine how well you play it. To help you in that area I suggest you stand a little taller at address than you normally do. By so doing you raise your eye level, which gives you a better view of the distance to be covered. This in turn helps you program more accurately the force of strike required. And, as a bonus, standing taller might help you swing the putter more freely and fully.

Should you putt or chip from the fringe of the green? A lot depends, of course, on ground and grass conditions, but I'll generally choose to putt if given half a chance. Why? Well, I've always remembered a statement Arnold Palmer made to me when I first came on tour. Said Arnold: "You'll find, Jack, that your worst putt will be as good as your best chip. In other words, if you get the ball only to within five feet of the cup from 50 feet with a putter, that's about as bad as you'll do. But you've got to hit a pretty good chip from 50 feet to get the ball that close to the hole." I've often reminded Arnold of this piece of advice—typical of the help he gave me—when I've seen him chip from the fringe!

J McQueen

SAND PLAY

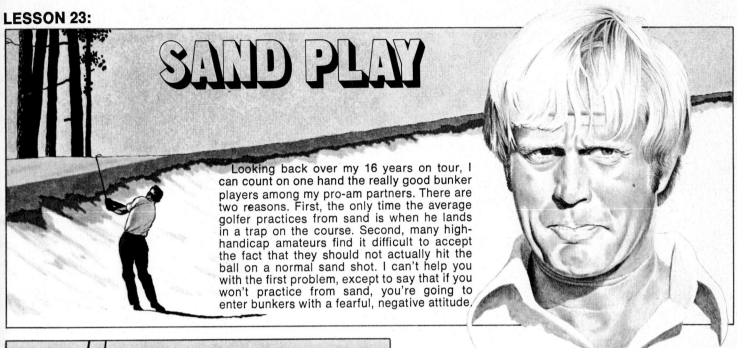

Looking back over my 16 years on tour, I can count on one hand the really good bunker players among my pro-am partners. There are two reasons. First, the only time the average golfer practices from sand is when he lands in a trap on the course. Second, many high-handicap amateurs find it difficult to accept the fact that they should not actually hit the ball on a normal sand shot. I can't help you with the first problem, except to say that if you won't practice from sand, you're going to enter bunkers with a fearful, negative attitude.

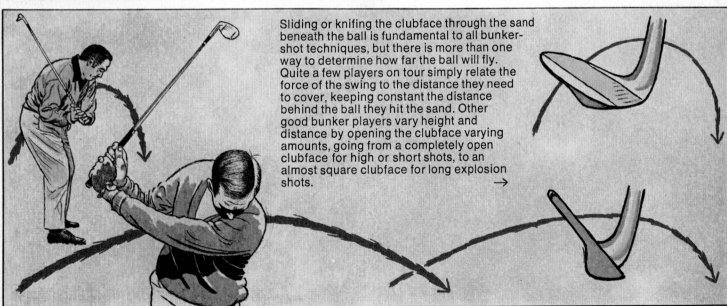

Problem No. 2 is easier to conquer. All it demands is a clear under-standing of the technology of sand play. If you will just keep in mind that hitting firmly into the sand a couple of inches behind the ball will create sufficient pressure to "explode" the ball out of the bunker, half your mental block will be cured. You will cure the other half simply by remembering *to hit through the sand without closing the clubface*. In other words, follow through without rolling your wrists.

To concentrate on the sand instead of the ball on normal trap shots, I envision an area about eight inches long and three inches wide, of which the ball is a part. As I set up to the shot I focus mentally on removing not only the ball but also the oblong of sand beneath it. If I achieve that objective there is no way I can leave the ball in the sand.

Sliding or knifing the clubface through the sand beneath the ball is fundamental to all bunker-shot techniques, but there is more than one way to determine how far the ball will fly. Quite a few players on tour simply relate the force of the swing to the distance they need to cover, keeping constant the distance behind the ball they hit the sand. Other good bunker players vary height and distance by opening the clubface varying amounts, going from a completely open clubface for high or short shots, to an almost square clubface for long explosion shots. →

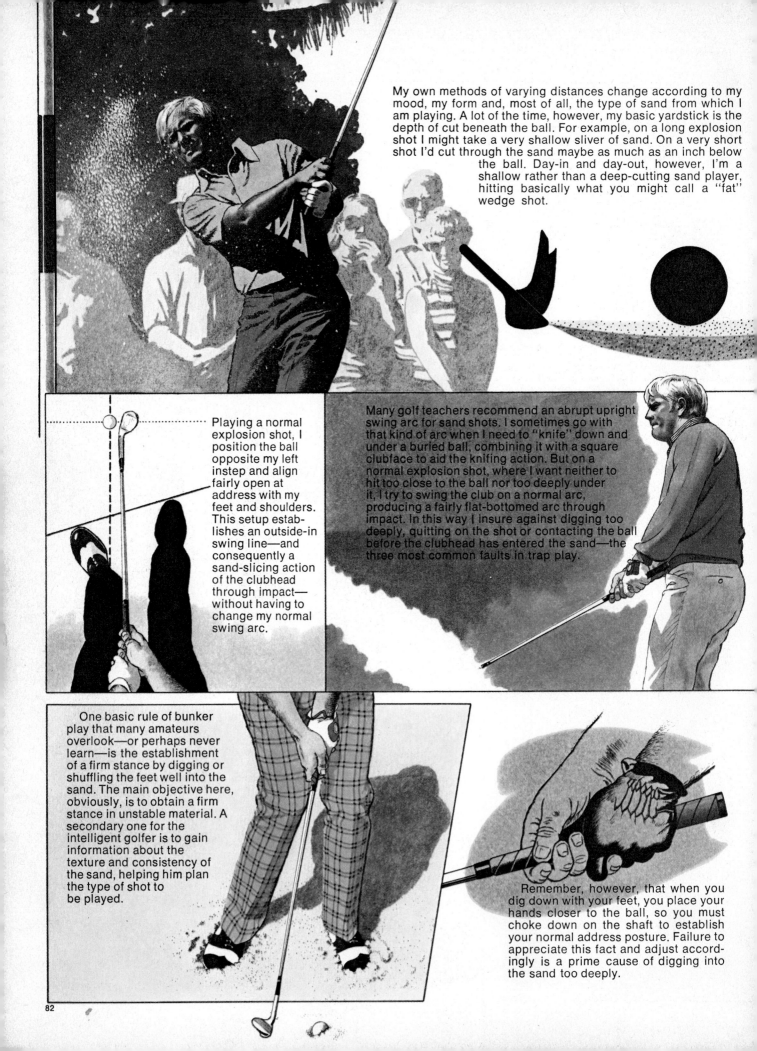

My own methods of varying distances change according to my mood, my form and, most of all, the type of sand from which I am playing. A lot of the time, however, my basic yardstick is the depth of cut beneath the ball. For example, on a long explosion shot I might take a very shallow sliver of sand. On a very short shot I'd cut through the sand maybe as much as an inch below the ball. Day-in and day-out, however, I'm a shallow rather than a deep-cutting sand player, hitting basically what you might call a "fat" wedge shot.

Playing a normal explosion shot, I position the ball opposite my left instep and align fairly open at address with my feet and shoulders. This setup establishes an outside-in swing line—and consequently a sand-slicing action of the clubhead through impact—without having to change my normal swing arc.

Many golf teachers recommend an abrupt upright swing arc for sand shots. I sometimes go with that kind of arc when I need to "knife" down and under a buried ball, combining it with a square clubface to aid the knifing action. But on a normal explosion shot, where I want neither to hit too close to the ball nor too deeply under it, I try to swing the club on a normal arc, producing a fairly flat-bottomed arc through impact. In this way I insure against digging too deeply, quitting on the shot or contacting the ball before the clubhead has entered the sand—the three most common faults in trap play.

One basic rule of bunker play that many amateurs overlook—or perhaps never learn—is the establishment of a firm stance by digging or shuffling the feet well into the sand. The main objective here, obviously, is to obtain a firm stance in unstable material. A secondary one for the intelligent golfer is to gain information about the texture and consistency of the sand, helping him plan the type of shot to be played.

Remember, however, that when you dig down with your feet, you place your hands closer to the ball, so you must choke down on the shaft to establish your normal address posture. Failure to appreciate this fact and adjust accordingly is a prime cause of digging into the sand too deeply.

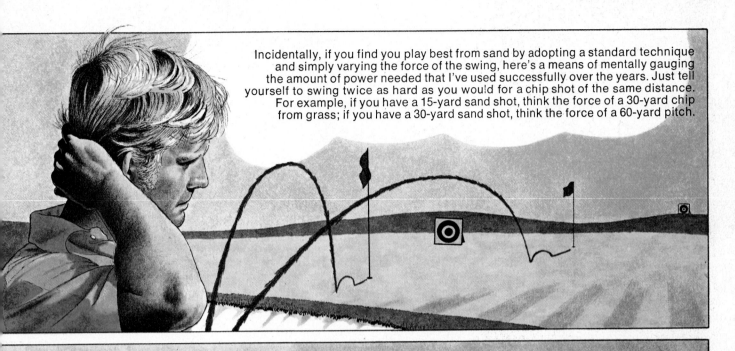

Incidentally, if you find you play best from sand by adopting a standard technique and simply varying the force of the swing, here's a means of mentally gauging the amount of power needed that I've used successfully over the years. Just tell yourself to swing twice as hard as you would for a chip shot of the same distance. For example, if you have a 15-yard sand shot, think the force of a 30-yard chip from grass; if you have a 30-yard sand shot, think the force of a 60-yard pitch.

To further promote the flat-bottomed swing arc that slides the clubhead shallowly through the sand beneath the ball, on most explosion shots I hit much earlier and more pronouncedly than usual with my right hand. The result of this is an early uncocking of the wrists—almost a "hit from the top"—that insures a complete release of the clubhead and a sweeping-through-the-sand rather than a digging-into-the-sand action.

Once you have become competent at removing the ball from sand, your expertise as a bunker player will depend on your willingness to practice and experiment with various lies, trajectories, types of spin and degrees of power. I use literally scores of variations on the basic theme of sliding the club through the sand beneath the ball.

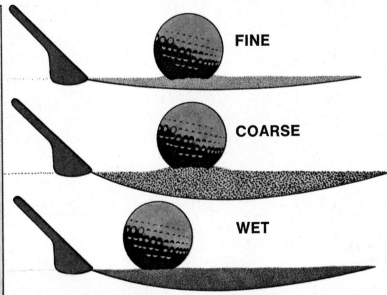

FINE

COARSE

WET

One key to becoming a good all-round trap player is the ability to cope with variations in sand texture. I classify sand broadly as fine, coarse and wet, and I play my best from wet sand because it allows the club to bounce easily, minimizing the need for a precise depth of cut. Coarse sand is a little more demanding, but its bounce-promoting qualities still make it comparatively simple to play. For me—and I believe most other golfers—fine sand poses the biggest problem, because its limited resistance to the clubhead promotes digging too deeply.

Incidentally, relating to bounce, I do not subscribe to the popular belief that the ideal sand wedge possesses an extremely deep, wide flange. Granted this type of club will perform beautifully from perfect lies, but how many perfect lies do you encounter in bunkers? To me, a far more effective club to cope with all the variations is a wedge with only a medium-deep flange. This allows for variations in the depth of cut that are almost impossible with a very deep-flanged club.

Finally, here is perhaps the most valuable tip I can give to any golfer having bunker problems. There is a definite tendency any time you land in sand to rush the shot. It's almost a psychological reflex in some players, bred of fear, lack of experience and an instinctive desire to get through an ugly moment as fast as possible. The result invariably is a tense lurch or chop at the ball which usually compounds the disaster.

If you see yourself here, determine that in the future you will play every bunker shot *in slow motion*. I guarantee that if you can maintain a slow-motion tempo, mentally and physically, from start to finish, you must improve your sand play.

An open setup, an upright swing path and a somewhat open clubface are basic requirements of most green-side bunker shots. But even these won't work consistently without enough practice to overcome the inherent fear of sand that afflicts most high handicappers.

PART 5: SPECIAL SHOTMAKING TECHNIQUES

INCREASE YOUR POWER

Physical strength is not the key to distance in golf. There are a number of players on the tour physically stronger than me who seldom drive the ball past me.

I believe the three big factors determining how far you hit the ball are width of clubhead arc, degree of body coil in the backswing, and quality of leg and hip action in the downswing.

Of course there are other factors—for instance, you'll never hit the ball far unless you strike it squarely. But, assuming you make decent contact most of the time, if you want more distance you should think in terms of lengthening your clubhead arc, or increasing your backswing body coil, or sharpening up your lower body downswing action—or all three.

If you decide to try for a bigger arc by swinging on a more upright path, the danger at first might be a tendency to sway or lift your shoulders instead of coiling them and stretching your arms. To prevent such movement, "grip" the ground with your spikes, and keep your head still, as you S-T-R-E-T-C-H the clubhead away from the ball in a smooth, "one-piece" movement of the clubhead, arms, shoulders and hips.

To achieve a true coiling—rather than a weak spinning—action, you must, of course, anchor your lower body as a resistance to the turning motion of your shoulders. The right knee is the secret here. It is vital that it remain flexed throughout the backswing, otherwise all kinds of faults will develop. Your left heel may leave the ground as you complete the backswing, but it should be **dragged** up by the stretching effect of your body coiling, never lifted deliberately. If you are supple enough to simply roll onto the inside of the foot without its leaving the ground, so much the better.

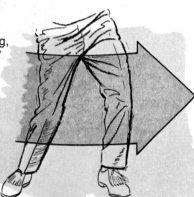

This lower-body action is very simple to describe. As you complete the backswing, your legs drive laterally towards the target.

Simultaneously, turn your hips toward the target, continuing to do so without pause to the completion of the swing.

My "flying right elbow" and "upright" plane have sometimes been criticized as poor backswing form. Well, I could change both —but if I did, I'd certainly lose distance.

So long as my right elbow and forearm point more or less downward at the top of my backswing, I don't care how high the elbow "flies." Allowing it to move well away from my side enables me to achieve a big, wide clubhead arc. Hugging the elbow to my side would limit my arc, and thus my power.

I also favor a fairly upright swing plane to widen my arc. Stretching the club straight back from the ball as far as possible, without swaying, then stretching it as high as possible, gives me a much fuller arc than I would achieve by swinging more around my body on a flatter plane.

Nobody ever hit a golf ball far without fully coiling his body on the backswing. With the driver, I feel that I coil my shoulders, hips and arms about as far around as they will physically go.

I know it is unfashionable today to talk of turning the hips, but I believe the hips **must** turn to allow the shoulders to coil fully on a driver swing. Trying to over-restrict their hip-turn causes many golfers to make no body turn at all, which is worse than too much body turn. Your shoulders should actually **out-turn** your hips. But if you can't make a decent shoulder turn without letting your hips turn fully, then let them turn. So long as this hip turn doesn't cause your right leg to stiffen, it will do little harm compared to the effect no body turn will have on reducing your distance.

The third critical factor in long-hitting is leverage—the last-minute release of the clubhead into the ball by the uncocking of the wrists.

All long drivers restrain this wrist release—in which the clubhead travels many feet while the hands travel inches—to the very last split second. They do so by starting the down-swing with their legs and hips.

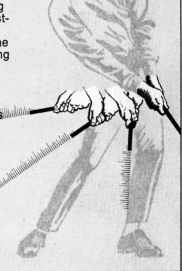

Many golfers actually ruin their chance of hitting a long ball by **trying** to do so. They submit to the almost irresistable urge to lash the clubhead into the ball with their hands. This **always** reduces distance, (1) by preventing accurate delivery of the clubface, and (2) by uncocking the wrists too early, dissipating the tremendous clubhead speed that comes from their properly-timed leverage of the clubhead through the ball.

Assuming you have a basically sound swing and a smooth tempo, the faster you use your legs and hips in the down-swing, the greater the leverage you will generate, and the farther you will hit the ball.

FOR CRISPER IRONS...

Many golfers who hit their woods decently play relatively poorly with the irons because they steer or jab at the ball with these clubs. "Accuracy-anxiety" is their prime problem—over-concern with direction and landing the ball on target instead of **SWINGING** the club **THROUGH** the ball **TO** the target. Remember that any kind of a steering motion is likely to disrupt both your arc and clubface alignment and thus misdirect the shot. With every iron in the bag you must swing the clubhead **FREELY** and **CONFIDENTLY**. Don't worry about the outcome of the shot until the ball is on its way.

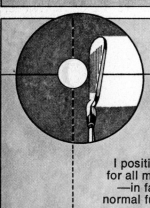

I position the ball for all my iron shots —in fact, all my normal full golf shots —opposite my left heel. It is at this point in my swing that the cluhbead is traveling along the target line.

If I positioned the ball farther back toward my right heel, I'd push the ball to the right because the clubhead would still be moving in that direction from inside the target line, during impact. If I positioned the ball farther forward, the clubhead would reach it after starting back to inside the target line. This would pull the ball. You should check at what point relative to **YOUR** feet, with **YOUR** swing, the clubhead travels straight along the target line.

But beware of moving onto your left side too violently. My way of preventing this is to feel that I stay on the **INSIDE** of my left foot through impact. Then my left foot rolls so that at the completion of the swing its outer part carries 95 per cent of my weight.

On short irons—the 8, 9 and, particularly, the wedge—I let my weight favor my left foot at address and throughout the backswing. This establishes a steeper down-and-through swing, which I desire with short irons.

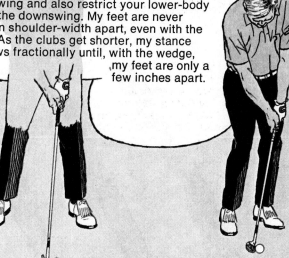

Avoid too wide a stance on your iron shots. It could set up a lateral sway instead of a turn on the backswing and also restrict your lower-body action on the downswing. My feet are never more than shoulder-width apart, even with the driver. As the clubs get shorter, my stance narrows fractionally until, with the wedge, my feet are only a few inches apart.

Your stance with every club should be wide enough to give you good balance, but not so wide as to restrict your body turn. The shorter the shot the less body movement you need. This reduces the problem of balance and allows a narrower stance.

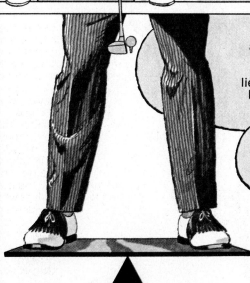

You hear a lot of conflicting advice about weight distribution, especially for iron shots. I like to keep things simple. For **ALL** shots from a level lie, from the 1-iron through the 7-iron, I distribute my weight at address not only equally between both feet, but equally between the balls and heels of each foot. Distributing weight unequally at address would disrupt my balance.

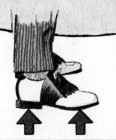

However you like to distribute your weight at address, it is vital that at impact, on every iron shot, it be mostly on your left foot. If it isn't, you cannot swing correctly down and through the ball with the clubhead striking in the ball-turf sequence essential to strong iron play.

To hit good iron shots it is imperative that the hands lead the clubhead through the ball. I set up at address to encourage this action. By establishing a straight line with my left arm and club shaft from my left shoulder to the ball, I insure that my hands are slightly ahead of the ball at address. They thus have the best chance of returning there at impact.

Normally I don't ground my clubhead for a fairway iron shot, for three reasons. First, I avoid a penalty stroke if the ball should accidentally move while I'm preparing to swing. Second, I avoid any tendency to stub the club on the ground during my takeaway. Third, I am able to start my swing the same way every time. Most golfers can learn quickly to start back without first soling the club. I believe their backswings would become more consistent and fluid if they developed this technique.

Head movement up and down can be a worse shot-wrecker than lateral swaying, especially on iron shots where you have less margin for error in striking than when the ball sits on a tee. If your head goes down in the backswing and up in the downswing, you'll top a lot of shots. If it goes up in the backswing and down in the downswing, you'll frequently hit the ground before the ball. So make a conscious effort to maintain a **LEVEL** head throughout your swing.

Much the same sort of thing applies to yo left arm. As the length of the shot and the clu shaft decrease, there's a tendency to let t left arm get lazy and bend during the swin Don't. If it stays bent through i pact, you risk topping the ball it straightens on the downswir most likely you'll catch the grou behind the ball by lengthening t radius of your swing.

How far back should you swing each iron? I can't answer that—only you can. The important factors are how much you can wind up your body without swaying or spinning it and how high you can swing your hands without bending your left arm or loosening your grip on the club. Practice will tell you the answer. Once you know it—and the distance you can hit each club—select clubs that allow you to make your **FULL NATURAL** swing with every iron. That way you eliminate the mental and physical variables inherent in half- and three-quarter shots, and you breed repetition.

A question I'm often asked: how much power goes into a long-iron shot compared to a short-iron shot? Answer: the same amount. I apply uniform power through the ball with **ALL** the irons. My swing merely becomes a little longer with any increased length of club. Next time you practice, hit a few 9-iron shots, then pick up your 2-iron and swing with the same amount of power.

Many golfers have trouble with the longer irons because they swing down too steeply on these shots. They either stick the club in the ground or hit "fat" behind the ball. You must **SWEEP** the ball away with these clubs. In setting up to a long iron shot, think "driver swing." Try to sweep the clubhead through the ball so that it just clips the grass after impact, instead of actually taking a divot.

J. McQueen

It's worth making the point again that your basic golf swing should not change just because the club in your hands does. The length of your shaft will automatically determine how far you stand from the ball if you've developed a sound swing, and the longer the shaft the bigger the arc you'll draw. Everything else—including the amount of power you apply on all normal shots—should remain the same.

LESSON 26:
DRIVING TECHNIQUE

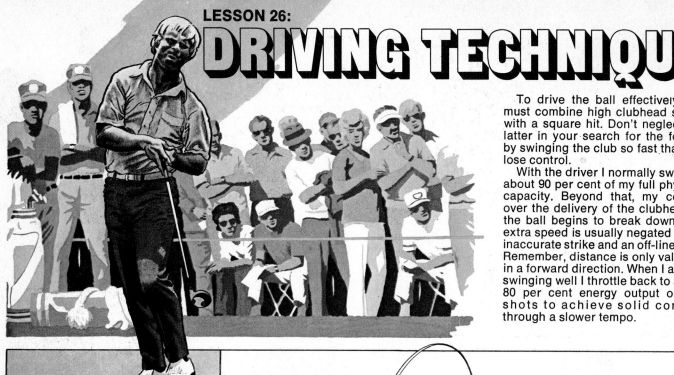

To drive the ball effectively you must combine high clubhead speed with a square hit. Don't neglect the latter in your search for the former by swinging the club so fast that you lose control.

With the driver I normally swing at about 90 per cent of my full physical capacity. Beyond that, my control over the delivery of the clubhead to the ball begins to break down. The extra speed is usually negated by an inaccurate strike and an off-line shot. Remember, distance is only valuable in a forward direction. When I am not swinging well I throttle back to about 80 per cent energy output on tee shots to achieve solid contact through a slower tempo.

Be certain you get a driver that matches your swing characteristics, particularly your tempo. Find a club with a flex pattern complementary to your timing, one that delivers the clubhead squarely to the ball without need for swing compensations. If you swing hard and fast you will normally need a relatively stiff-shafted club— too much flex will leave the clubface open at impact. For the slow or easy swinger a relatively "soft" shaft usually helps promote square delivery of the clubface.

Unless wind conditions dictate otherwise I drive for carry rather than run, which means I hit the ball high. There are no hazards in the air and a high-flying, soft-landing ball gives me maximum control over placement of the tee shot. I recommend a similar policy for golfers to whom distance isn't a problem. But if you lack length, you're generally going to be better off driving for run rather than height. To develop this you must learn to draw the ball from right to left.

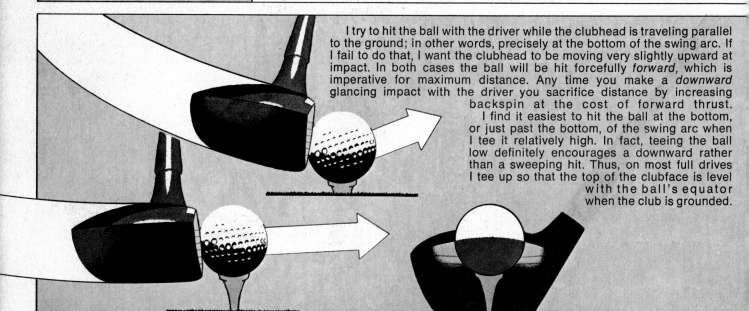

I try to hit the ball with the driver while the clubhead is traveling parallel to the ground; in other words, precisely at the bottom of the swing arc. If I fail to do that, I want the clubhead to be moving very slightly upward at impact. In both cases the ball will be hit forcefully *forward*, which is imperative for maximum distance. Any time you make a *downward* glancing impact with the driver you sacrifice distance by increasing backspin at the cost of forward thrust.

I find it easiest to hit the ball at the bottom, or just past the bottom, of the swing arc when I tee it relatively high. In fact, teeing the ball low definitely encourages a downward rather than a sweeping hit. Thus, on most full drives I tee up so that the top of the clubface is level with the ball's equator when the club is grounded.

The long drivers on tour are the golfers who *swing* the club-head through the ball fast and freely. This does not — as many amateurs seem to think — require a great amount of George Foreman-type physical strength. What it does demand is a swing pattern that develops a high degree of leverage. Once that pattern has been developed, its day-to-day effectiveness depends on muscular coordination, not muscular strength.

For most shots, I position my right foot square (at right angles) to my target line, but when driving I point this foot a few degrees to the right of that position. Reason? I can make a fuller and freer upper body turn and thus generate a little extra clubhead speed through greater leverage. Try this yourself if you have difficulty "coiling the spring" fully going back.

If your problem is the reverse — plenty of turn but sluggish leg-hip action starting down — open up your left foot by angling it a few degrees more toward the target than usual. You'll find that this will facilitate a faster and freer unwinding of the lower body throughout the downswing. Usually with the driver my left foot is angled about 45 degrees toward the target to insure that my legs and hips initiate my downswing.

It is important on all shots to hit *through*, not *at*, the ball. At no time is this more true than when using the driver. If you have difficulty achieving this, try focusing your mind on generating maximum clubhead speed *throughout the entire impact zone*, rather than at the ball. In other words "hit through" the area three feet behind and three feet beyond the ball.

In modern swing methodology there is much talk about "hitting late" with the hands and wrists—delaying their release as long as possible during the downswing. Well, I'd never drive the ball as far as I do if I went at tee-shots with that kind of thought. To me, *so long as the legs work first starting the downswing* it's impossible to hit "too early" with the hands and wrists. They aren't held back in any way.

On the same tack, you hear a lot of talk about "left-sidedness" versus "right-sidedness." To me, you can't use your right side too much *so long as your left side leads and controls the swing*. For example, I hit just about as hard as I can with my right hand on full drives. Trouble only occurs if my left hand isn't leading and controlling the swing.

I have three ways of generating extra yardage when a situation calls for a particularly big drive.
1. Preparing to tee off, I consciously try to get myself into big-hit condition by letting my muscles go loose and easy. Then I am a little less deliberate in standing up to the ball, and I hit before tension can begin to build up. I use this device primarily when accuracy is not a factor and I am really intent on "flat-outing" a drive.

2. When both accuracy and extra distance are factors, my primary thought is to make a particularly slow and smooth "one-piece" takeaway. By so doing I eliminate rush — the biggest danger when you're going for a big one — and establish a smooth tempo for the swing. A deliberate start-back also insures that I'll complete my backswing before I start my downswing, which guarantees maximum leverage and clubhead speed.

3. My third means of producing extra distance is to speed up my hip action on the downswing. The way I play golf, the faster my hips turn and clear from the top of the swing the greater the leverage I generate and the faster the clubhead travels. Here the critical factor is accelerating the hip turn while keeping the whole action smooth. Any jerkiness will inevitably cause a bad shot.

Golfers who have distance problems from the tee, yet are unable to make a bigger body turn without losing swing control, might find they can increase the arc of the swing — and thus their yardage potential — by swinging their arms higher going back. I often make a particular point with the driver of "reaching for the clouds" with my hands. In addition to extending my arc, this also helps me complete my backswing before I start my downswing — an absolute requisite for maximum leverage.

If you want distance, don't forget to *hit through* the ball with the *clubhead*. I've never seen a big hitter yet who "let the clubhead do the work." What I have seen when a player really moves it out there is a fast, free and *smooth* swing of the clubhead *through* the ball, usually motivated by excellent body leverage.

PART 6: TROUBLE SHOTS

LESSON 27:
GRASSES

My favorite fairway grass is sand-based fescue, a very soft-bladed growth that is universal to the great British links courses. It is almost self-maintaining, and it is a wonderful surface for iron shots, but it is rare in the U.S.—chiefly because it requires a temperate climate. My next favorites are close-cropped hybrid Bermuda and poa annua. The latter is much-maligned because of its clumpiness when it invades other types of greens, but is excellent for well-maintained fairways.

When finely mowed, Berm grass—whether common hybrid—offers the good go perhaps the best of all fairv surfaces in the U.S. It allo maximum manipulation of ball through the applicat of backspin and sides resulting from cl striking and the f "gripping" of the against a tough, resili surface. That's why favorite practice tu close-cropped Bermu

One reason many fairways are kept comparatively long is that handicap players feel more confident when the ball sits on a lush bed of grass rather than tight to the ground. I'll give you another reason to vote for lush fairways if you're on your club's greens committee. The more grass between the club and ball at impact, the less the shot will be affected by sidespin, and therefore the less mis-hit shots will slice or hook.

Grass type and condition should be a factor in you strategical approach to shot placement. Fo example, in the South and Southwest, common Bermuda often ind cates an old course, which frequently means hard ground. If the gras is then cut low, you can anticipate a lot of run. The same applies wit fescue on the rare occasions it is found in the U.S. Conversely, hybri Bermudas, bluegrass, poa annua and most northern bent grasses te toward lushness, especially during summer when they demand hea watering. Thus the ball will generally settle close to where it lands, which requires maximum carry through the air.

As a further safeguard against sticking the club in the ground when playing from Bermuda, in recent years I've worked at reducing my wrist action on short pitch shots. The feel I strive for back and through is a firm sweep action of the hands, wrists and arms working as a unit. Practicing this stroke to the new green in my back yard, I try to avoid taking a proper divot, simply grazing the grass as I sweep the ball into the air.

In chipping and putting remember that all Bermud grasses grow toward th setting sun. Thus, you' usually be playing against the grain—and most Ber mudas have pronounce grain—when you're hittin toward the east. A furthe clue to the grain is th appearance of the grass When it looks shiny, th grain is away from you When it looks dull, th grain is toward you.

For the less skilled golfer, the seemingly tight lies presented by short-cut or dormant Bermuda often present the problem of "hitting fat" that can quickly destroy confidence. One answer for the regular Bermuda player is to be sure that he uses clubs with adequate "bounce" built into the soles. Another answer, although really of a Band-Aid nature, is to increase the chance of catching the ball cleanly by moving it back slightly at address. However, if you try this, allow for a tendency to hook.

Like common Bermuda, poa annua cut every day in hot season offers an excellent fairway surface. When either becomes too long and lush, the good golfer risks getting "flyers" or "squirters" on many iron shots—a frequent problem for tournament players when the tour heads north into bent and bluegrass country.

Under those conditions, I go to much the same strategy and technique I use for semirough. First, I go up one club—take, say, an 8-iron for normal 7-iron distance. Then, to overcome the ball's "hot" landing speed and lack of spin, I try to hit it as high as possible by sweeping through it with a "dead-wrists" action.

If you need distance from a lush or soft-grass fairway (i.e., bent, bluegrass or poa annua), try punching the ball instead of sweeping it away. Hit down on it hard with your right hand and the ball will really squirt forward low and hard, giving you maybe as much as three clubs' more distance. But remember that it will also run a mile, and make allowance.

Forethought is needed in pitching and chipping to Bermuda greens. You will rarely get much run on well-kept hybrid Bermuda, which necessitates flying the ball well up to the pin. Close-cropped common Bermuda sometimes offers more run, especially when the ground is hard. But, generally, the pitch-and-run shot is tricky on Bermuda greens.

Because of the thick root system and tough runners, there is always a risk of leaving the club in the ground when pitching and chipping from Bermuda. The soundest way to prevent this is to develop a firm, positive backswing from which the clubhead can be crisply *accelerated* through the ball.

Softer northern grasses like bent and poa annua have less grain, but what there is will generally run in the direction of drainage—toward the nearest low-lying land. That's why I usually take a good look at the surrounding territory as I walk onto these types of greens.

On most Bermuda greens, I try in putting to catch the ball slightly on the upstroke. This type of stroke gets the ball rolling truly end over end faster and better than a downward motion of the putter blade. Also, by hitting slightly upward I guard against catching the grass before the ball, which on Bermuda will always decelerate the putterhead and twist its face off line.

LESSON 28:

HILLY LIES

Golf would certainly be a easier game if the world we dead flat, but it would also b incredibly dull. So dor bemoan those angled lie Accept them as a part the natural challenge golf, and tackle the with a positive attitud

My prime objective in playing uphill and downhill lies is to allow myself to swing as normally as possible by positioning myself as perpendicular to the slope as possible. Set up thus, my clubhead will naturally follow the slope of the ground—going back low and rising coming through on an uphill lie, and rising quickly but coming through low on a downhill lie. By setting up this way, I reduce the chances of catching the ground before the ball on an uphill lie, and catching the ball "thin" or even topping it on a downhill lie.

With the ball above one's feet, the natural (and in this case correct) tendency is to stand more erect than usual and—depending on the severity of slope—to choke down on the club. In my case, setting my weight more toward my toes helps me to retain balance. So does a special effort to swing smoothly and compactly, with a mental picture of "sweeping" the ball away cleanly, rather than digging it out of the hillside. Generally—especially from a severe slope—I will go with the tendency of the ball to draw, and simply aim accordingly at address.

With the ball below one feet, the natural tendency is bend more than usual at the kne and/or waist. I also like to grip club as close to its end as possi in order to keep it as close as possible to its normal distance the ball. To preserve my balanc I set most of my weight on my heels, and again try to swing as smoothly and compactly as poss I find it particularly vital on this shot to keep my head very still. I retain my knee flex well into th follow-through. When the slope severe, I simply allow for the ba to fade and change my address alignment accordingly.

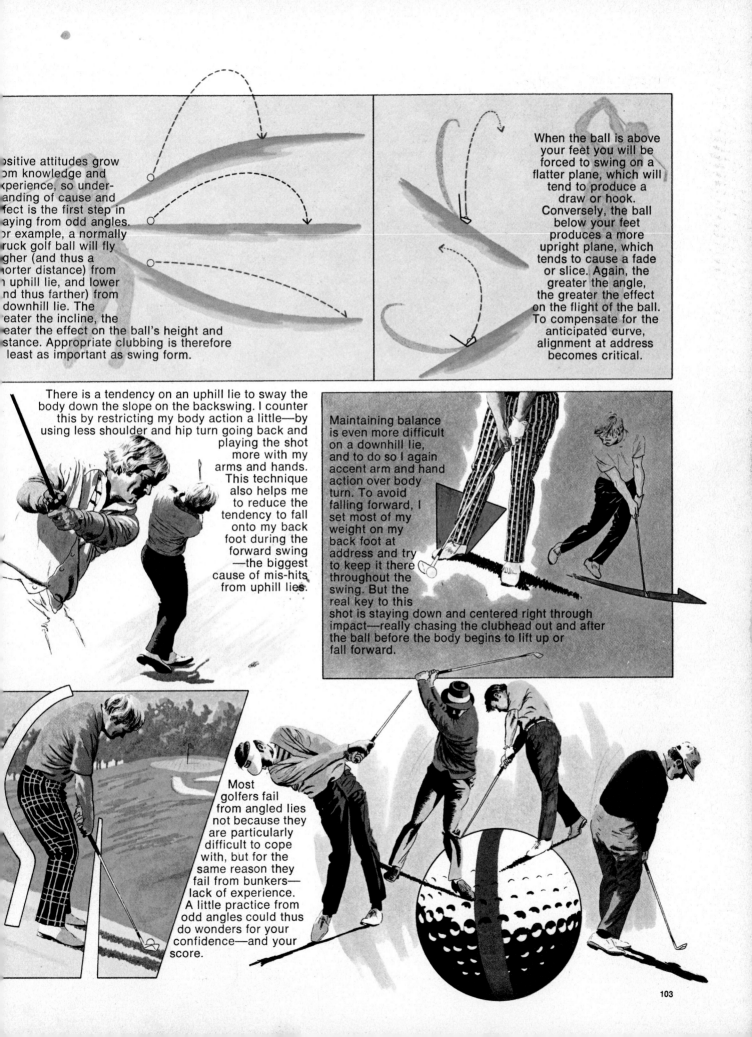

ositive attitudes grow om knowledge and xperience, so under- anding of cause and fect is the first step in aying from odd angles. or example, a normally ruck golf ball will fly gher (and thus a orter distance) from uphill lie, and lower nd thus farther) from downhill lie. The eater the incline, the eater the effect on the ball's height and stance. Appropriate clubbing is therefore least as important as swing form.

When the ball is above your feet you will be forced to swing on a flatter plane, which will tend to produce a draw or hook. Conversely, the ball below your feet produces a more upright plane, which tends to cause a fade or slice. Again, the greater the angle, the greater the effect on the flight of the ball. To compensate for the anticipated curve, alignment at address becomes critical.

There is a tendency on an uphill lie to sway the body down the slope on the backswing. I counter this by restricting my body action a little—by using less shoulder and hip turn going back and playing the shot more with my arms and hands. This technique also helps me to reduce the tendency to fall onto my back foot during the forward swing —the biggest cause of mis-hits from uphill lies.

Maintaining balance is even more difficult on a downhill lie, and to do so I again accent arm and hand action over body turn. To avoid falling forward, I set most of my weight on my back foot at address and try to keep it there throughout the swing. But the real key to this shot is staying down and centered right through impact—really chasing the clubhead out and after the ball before the body begins to lift up or fall forward.

Most golfers fail from angled lies not because they are particularly difficult to cope with, but for the same reason they fail from bunkers— lack of experience. A little practice from odd angles could thus do wonders for your confidence—and your score.

PLAYING FROM ROUGH

Many amateurs tend to lose their wits when they leave the fairway. It's as important to coolly pre-plan trouble shots as it is drives and approaches from closely-mown turf — more important, in fact, because of the risk of further compounding your original error. Basically, I play two types of full shots from rough, and I always go at them with a clear mental picture of which one I'm attempting.

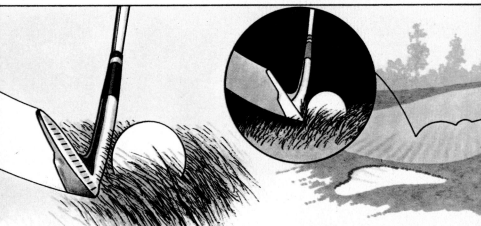

When you plan to punch a ball out of rough or under wind you'll certainly increase your control and improve your chance of sharp clubhead delivery by choking down on the shaft. On the other hand, you'll find that full use of the shaft facilitates the slow and easy swing tempo necessary to play *soft shots* — especially from long grass. The trick here is to make a full but *deliberate* swing, and in my case that requires all the distance I can put between my hands and the clubhead.

Understand how the direction of grass growth can affect your recovery shots. Grass growing away from the target will tend to check and close the clubface, so take more club than normal. Grass growing toward the target offers less resistance, but the ball will tend to "fly" because grass between it and the clubface at impact diminishes backspin. Thus, you should take less club than normal and allow for plenty of run.

On the rare occasions when I take a wood from a rugged rough lie, I usually try to play a special kind of shot that I first developed as an amateur. Starting with an open clubface, I try to make an even more upright swing than normal, then hit abruptly down into the ball by pulling downward hard with my left arm while hitting sharply with my right hand. This technique will also work well from hard ground, from "cuppy" fairway lies, and even from divot holes. Generally the ball does not fade as much from rough, using this action, as it would from the fairway. But allow for a little left-to-right bend just to be on the safe side.

One is a high-flying, soft-landing shot designed to stop quickly even though the intervention of grass between the clubface and the ball robs it of full back-spin. I achieve this type of shot by playing the ball forward in my stance, opening the clubface and sweeping the clubhead through impact with plenty of right hand "throwing" action.

My other basic rough shot is a low-flying, fast runner played when I want maximum distance. For this I employ a punching-type technique—ball back, hands forward, clubface square to slightly closed, steep backswing and downswing, and a determined effort to keep my left hand leading the clubhead through impact.

There's no doubt that, unless you are unusually strong, you'll do better from rough with a 4- or 5-wood than a long iron. The reason is simply that the rounded soles of the well-lofted woods cut through the grass more easily and cleanly than the straight, sharp leading edges of long irons.

The best way to cope with trouble is to stay out of it as much as possible, and the place to start doing that is on the tee. Always try to place your ball for the drive so that you can hit away from the worst trouble areas. If there are thick woods or deep grass to the left of the fairway, but relatively clear ground to the right, hit from the left side of the tee—away from the big trouble area.

When you're confronted with a lie well below foot level—as, say, in a gully or ditch — I recommend that you resist the natural inclination to get the club down to ball level by bending exaggeratedly at the knees. Instead, take a wider than normal stance and *bend from the waist* until the club can address the ball. You'll give yourself much more room and freedom to swing the club from this set-up than from a cramped, knees-bent posture.

A good example of how brains count as much as brawn in recovery play occurs when there is an inviting opening to a green but big trouble behind it. If, say, a 5-iron is the club you'd normally take for the distance, consider where the ball will finish if you hit a "flyer." Then take a 6- or 7-iron, which will get you home if it really "flies" and runs, or leave you with a simple chip if it doesn't.

105

LESSON 30:
TROUBLE SHOTS

Occasionally you will face situations where the only sane way out is to take an unplayable-lie penalty and drop clear, but don't give up without considering all the options. Many times during my career I've saved shots by playing left-handed (as when the ball is against a tree or fence), bouncing the ball back into play off a wall or other obstacle, or simply knocking the ball clear of trouble with the putter when there was no room to swing with any other club.

In playing from twigs, leaves, pine needles or similar loose materials, try to avoid grounding the club as you set up to the shot, thereby minimizing the risk of incurring a penalty for moving the ball. On full shots where the lie is clean the ball will usually behave much as it does from the fairway, so swing normally. Around the green loose materials usually react like soft sand, so consider playing a bunker shot.

Find it difficult to achieve good contact with the ball when forced to make a restricted backswing? The reason probably is that you concentrate on the awkward lie rather than on the execution of the swing. Next time you get in this fix, make sufficient practice swings to get a good feel for the swing you're about to make, then concentrate on making it.

Beware of clover, even in the fairway. It is a highly slick substance and when it gets between the club-face and the ball it invariably reduces backspin and produces a "flyer." Often from clover lies—as from thick, wet fairway grass—I'll play a choked-down, punched, running approach rather than gamble with the amount of "fly" I might get playing an orthodox full shot.

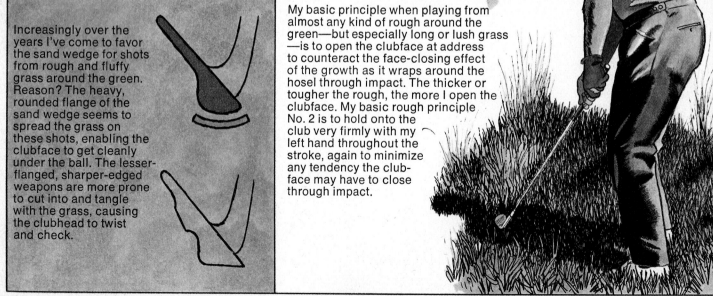

Increasingly over the years I've come to favor the sand wedge for shots from rough and fluffy grass around the green. Reason? The heavy, rounded flange of the sand wedge seems to spread the grass on these shots, enabling the clubface to get cleanly under the ball. The lesser-flanged, sharper-edged weapons are more prone to cut into and tangle with the grass, causing the clubhead to twist and check.

My basic principle when playing from almost any kind of rough around the green—but especially long or lush grass —is to open the clubface at address to counteract the face-closing effect of the growth as it wraps around the hosel through impact. The thicker or tougher the rough, the more I open the clubface. My basic rough principle No. 2 is to hold onto the club very firmly with my left hand throughout the stroke, again to minimize any tendency the club-face may have to close through impact.

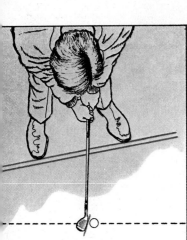

...should know that shots off hard...are ground generally fly lower and...farther than normal. To counter-...this, take less club and/or open...clubface and aim left at address...an intentional fade.

Landing in divot holes distresses many golfers more than it need. There are basically two ways to overcome the problem. The first, to be adopted when you can run the ball into the green, is to play a punch shot—ball back, club-face square, hands ahead of ball at address and impact, early pick-up, three-quarter swing, firm downward hit, no rolling of wrists until well beyond impact. In method No. 2, essential when the ball must fly to the target, move the ball forward, open the clubface, take a full swing and hit hard with the right hand through impact—again taking care not to roll the wrists until the ball is well on its way.

My best advice on playing a ball from water is don't, especially if it's completely submerged. However, if you do want to take the risk and don't mind getting wet, play the shot like a buried sand lie—clubface square or slightly closed, abrupt backswing and down-swing, and hard right-hand hit a couple of inches behind the ball. Use a 9-iron rather than a wedge; the smaller flange will slice through the water more easily.

...ying a high-flying, soft-landing...ch shot from the rough is never...sy, especially when you face an...ervening hazard and/or must...rk with a limited amount of...en. I mostly play these shots...e a soft blast from sand, open-...the clubface at address, pick-...the clubhead up sharply in...backswing, then dropping or...ding the clubhead under the...l. The key factor on this shot...ever to let the right hand roll...er the left through impact.

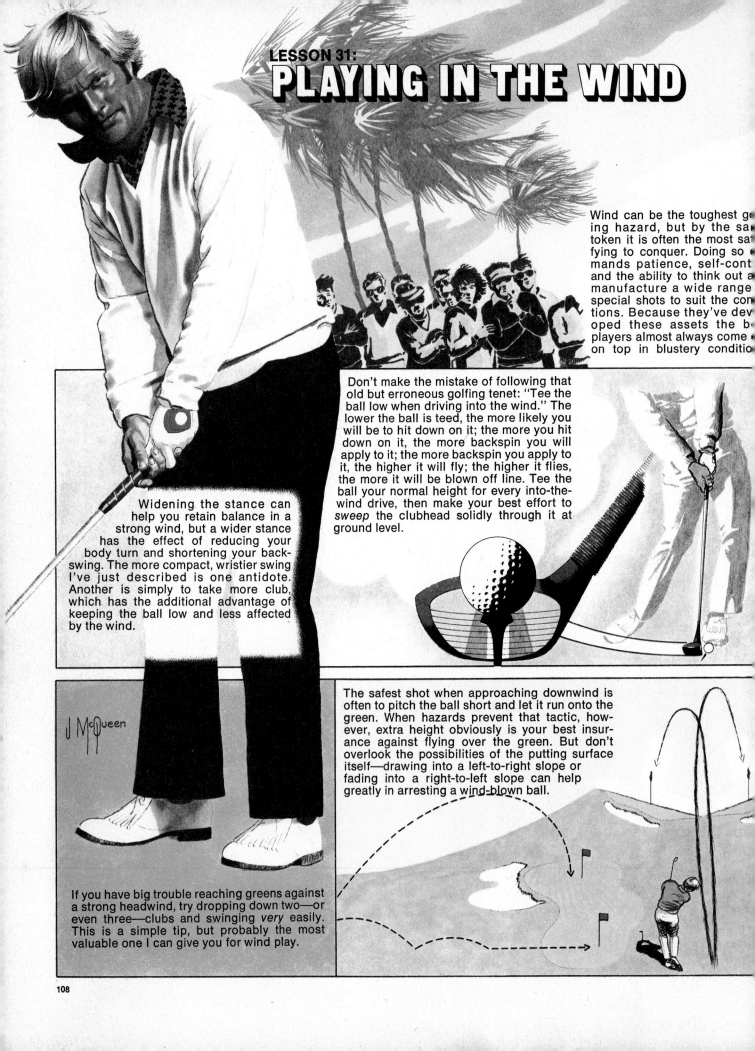

LESSON 31:
PLAYING IN THE WIND

Wind can be the toughest g[...] ing hazard, but by the sa[...] token it is often the most sa[...] fying to conquer. Doing so [...] mands patience, self-cont[...] and the ability to think out a[...] manufacture a wide range [...] special shots to suit the con[...] tions. Because they've dev[...] oped these assets the b[...] players almost always come [...] on top in blustery conditio[...]

Widening the stance can help you retain balance in a strong wind, but a wider stance has the effect of reducing your body turn and shortening your back-swing. The more compact, wristier swing I've just described is one antidote. Another is simply to take more club, which has the additional advantage of keeping the ball low and less affected by the wind.

J McQueen

If you have big trouble reaching greens against a strong headwind, try dropping down two—or even three—clubs and swinging *very* easily. This is a simple tip, but probably the most valuable one I can give you for wind play.

Don't make the mistake of following that old but erroneous golfing tenet: "Tee the ball low when driving into the wind." The lower the ball is teed, the more likely you will be to hit down on it; the more you hit down on it, the more backspin you will apply to it; the more backspin you apply to it, the higher it will fly; the higher it flies, the more it will be blown off line. Tee the ball your normal height for every into-the-wind drive, then make your best effort to *sweep* the clubhead solidly through it at ground level.

The safest shot when approaching downwind is often to pitch the ball short and let it run onto the green. When hazards prevent that tactic, how-ever, extra height obviously is your best insur-ance against flying over the green. But don't overlook the possibilities of the putting surface itself—drawing into a left-to-right slope or fading into a right-to-left slope can help greatly in arresting a wind-blown ball.

any golfers test wind strength and direction y tossing a pinch of grass in the air. Frequently the result fools them, because what's appening at near-ground-level is nothing ke what's happening aloft. To really check ut what the wind's going to do to your ball, ok up high—at the treetops or the clubouse flag, for example.

When wind, ground or weather conditions become so bad that I'd risk losing balance with my normal full swing, I generally seek more compactness of movement by employing less body and more hand action. I relax my wrists and allow them to break earlier and more fully in the backswing. This prompts a matching liveliness of wrist action through the ball.

a really powerful headind, when I want maximum distance or must mply get the ball to a eneral target area, I most always try to play draw shot. One reason that this shot will give e maximum roll. Anoth- is that the counterockwise sidespin that auses the ball to fly right left also produces a wer and a much more oring flight than the lefto-right sidespin that auses a faded shot.

In a big blow I always examine the possibility of hitting a driver "under" the wind from the fairway, rather than playing a high-soaring 3-wood shot. By gripping down an inch or two on the driver I can hit the ball 3-wood distance but much lower and under better control than would be possible with the 3-wood. Choking down does, of course, give you greater control and less height with every club in the bag—as long as you don't try to force the shot in a subconscious effort to counteract the shorter shaft.

here are two schools of thought among tour golfers about how to andle crosswinds. Some players prefer to combat the conditions by laying a draw into a left-to-right wind, and a fade into a right-to-left ind. Others like to go with the wind as much as possible, simply by iming off the line and letting the wind blow the ball back on target. ly tactics in a crosswind vary depending on its strength and the state f my game, but generally I will use the wind rather nan fight it. On long shots—particularly drives— idicious use of the wind can bring extra distance. or example, by teeing up on the left and hitting own the left side of the fairway in a left-to-right rosswind, you give the wind maximum chance o carry the ball while still keeping it in the airway.

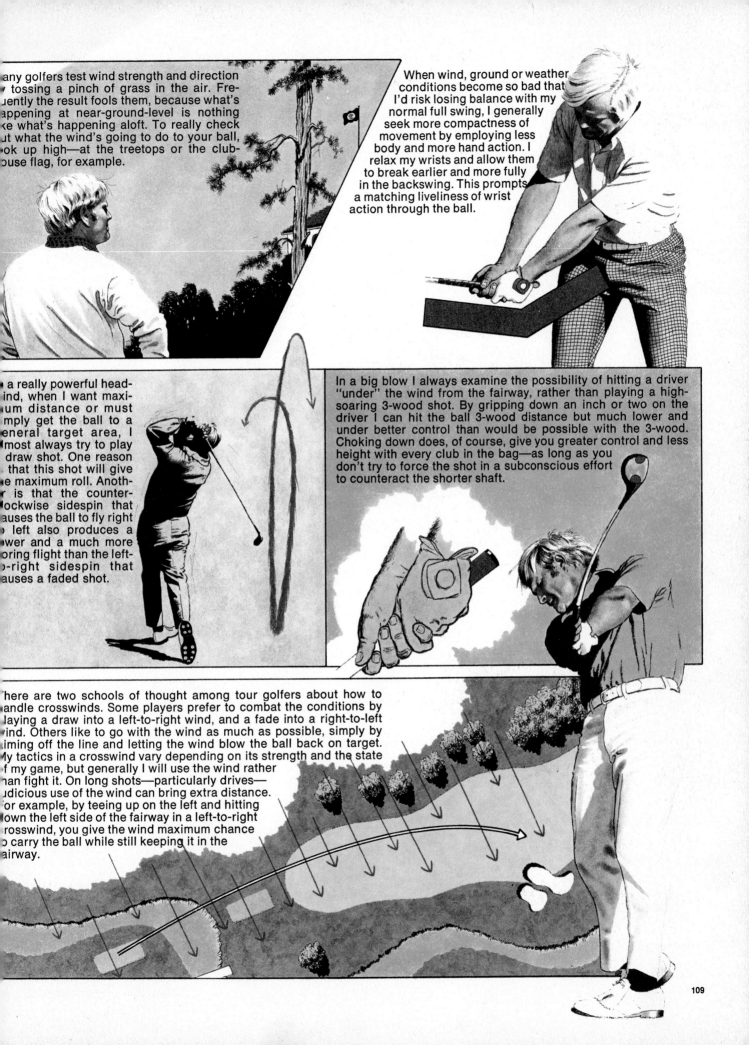

WET WEATHER GOLF

Golfers seem to respond to rough weather basically in three ways. One group simply stays home until the rain stops. Another group goes out and plays but with a negative attitude and usually a lot of griping and poor scores. The third group accepts the elements as just another variation in a multi-faceted game and responds with gusto to the special challenges they present. I belong to the third group—as any person dependent on golf for a living should.

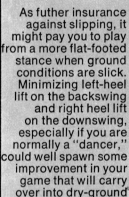
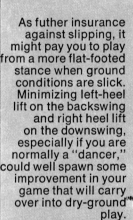

Ever notice how often tour players clean off their shoe spikes, especially when conditions underfoot are wet and sloppy? They do so to insure a firm footing, and you should do the same. Simply take a tee or a pitch-mark repairer and scrape any accumulations of mud or grass from your shoe soles prior to every shot on which you need solid contact with the ground.

As futher insurance against slipping, it might pay you to play from a more flat-footed stance when ground conditions are slick. Minimizing left-heel lift on the backswing and right heel lift on the downswing, especially if you are normally a "dancer," could well spawn some improvement in your game that will carry over into dry-ground play.

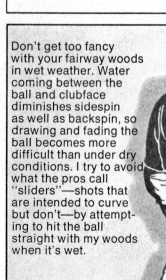

Don't get too fancy with your fairway woods in wet weather. Water coming between the ball and clubface diminishes sidespin as well as backspin, so drawing and fading the ball becomes more difficult than under dry conditions. I try to avoid what the pros call "sliders"—shots that are intended to curve but don't—by attempting to hit the ball straight with my woods when it's wet.

In wet or chilly weather dress as comfortably and protectively as possible and still allow myself maximum freedom of movement. That usually involves two or more layers of fairly light clothing rather than a single thick or heavy garment. Cashmere is my favorite anti-freeze material. If I'm forced to wear a rain jacket, I make sure it's plenty roomy around the shoulders and upper arms as well as light in weight. Even then I'll often remove it to play the big shots

Any form of really bad weather demands modifications not only in your technique but of your mental attitude. Perhaps the most critical mental adjustment most golfers need to make is learning to accept bad breaks and higher scores without losing their "cool."

Rhythm and tempo take on extra importance when you're being bullied by the elements. With rain running down your neck, you subconsciously risk hurrying both your setup and your swing. In those circumstances I try to make a conscious effort to get properly settled over the ball, then to swing as smoothly and fully as possible. Two of my key thoughts at such times are: "Make a *deliberate* takeaway" and "*Complete* the backswing."

Wet weather and wet ground conditions invariably produce "flyers" — shots that travel farther but bite less quickly than normal, due to reduced backspin caused by moisture on the ball and clubface. One obvious way to counteract this is to take less club, but a more sophisticated and reliable way is to fade the ball into the green. **The** extra height and spin resulting **from** a slight out-to-in cutting action will generally counter-balance the effects of a wet ball and clubface.

During the British Open, the mercury sometimes never gets out of the 50s and the wind-chill factor can make it feel like the 30s. My greatest concern if we face that sort of weather is to keep my hands warm. Depending on the temperature, I use my pockets, wear gloves between shots, or even employ a pair of handwarmers. Warm feet are almost as important to me as warm hands. I can't use my legs properly if my feet are numb. Two pairs of socks usually get the job done as long as my shoes are not too snug. For cold-spell tournaments, I usually pack a pair of old, stretched shoes to allow for extra foot insulation.

PART 7: STRATEGY

DRIVING STRATEGY

I am a "target" driver. I select and try to hit the ball to a specific section of the fairway, rather than just onto the fairway in general. One of the reasons I like to drive the ball high with a slight fade is the control this type of shot gives me in hitting specific targets.

The better a golf course is designed, the braver and more skillful a golfer must be to drive the ball to the ideal position for an approach shot. A perfect example is the 380-yard 13th hole at Pebble Beach, which couples a huge left-side fairway trap with a right-to-left sloping green. There is unlimited room to the right of the trap. But the golfer who doesn't analyze the hole, or who chickens out on the tee and drives right, will find it is almost impossible to stop the ball on the green coming in from the right. The closer to the trap you drive, the better your chances of stopping the second shot.

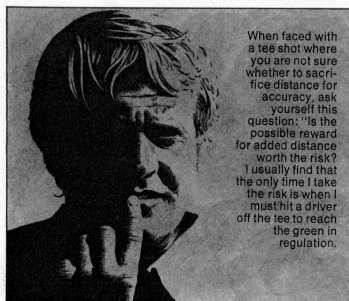

When faced with a tee shot where you are not sure whether to sacrifice distance for accuracy, ask yourself this question: "Is the possible reward for added distance worth the risk? I usually find that the only time I take the risk is when I must hit a driver off the tee to reach the green in regulation.

When you decide that the percentage shot is less than a full driver, the best stroke is a full swing with a 3-wood or long-iron—not an easy swing with the driver. Letting up with a driver almost always leads to quitting on the shot or an attempt to steer the ball into position with equally poor results.

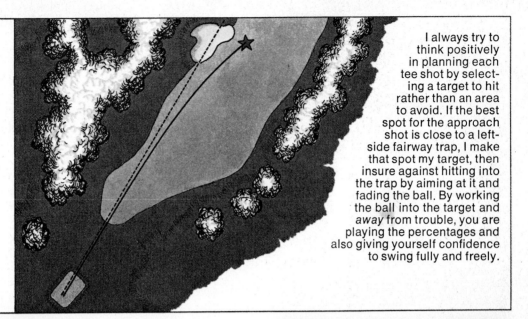

I rarely try to hit the ball dead straight with the driver. Having determined exactly where I want the ball to finish, I will play down either the left or right side of the fairway, fading or drawing the ball toward my target, depending on the configuration of the hole. Why? First, a straight shot is much more difficult to execute than a deliberate fade or draw. Second, by shaping shots as I've described I give myself the entire width of the fairway to play with, rather than the half-width I'd have if I aimed down the center and tried to hit straight.

I always try to think positively in planning each tee shot by selecting a target to hit rather than an area to avoid. If the best spot for the approach shot is close to a left-side fairway trap, I make that spot my target, then insure against hitting into the trap by aiming at it and fading the ball. By working the ball into the target and *away* from trouble, you are playing the percentages and also giving yourself confidence to swing fully and freely.

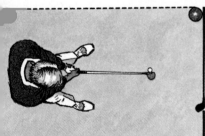

Playing for position—not distance—is the key to effective driving on nine out of 10 golf holes. It is virtually impossible to play for position, however, unless you know the approximate position of the pin on each hole. So don't miss any opportunities to note pin locations on holes you'll play later.

You often can gain an advantage on a blind dog-leg hole by discovering the pin position before teeing off. For example, when the pin on a dog-leg right is located on the right side of the green, the left side of the fairway usually affords the best approach angle. But when the pin is on the left side it might be better to cut the corner. You could have an open shot across the fairway even if you finish tight to the right.

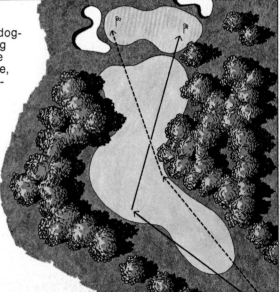

The first thing I look for on a tee is a level area large enough to accommodate me and the ball. Golf is difficult enough without playing your tee shots from angled lies. Remember you can tee up as far back as two club-lengths behind the markers.

Your natural fear of out-of-bounds areas will lessen considerably if you make a habit of teeing up as close as possible to the trouble area, then hitting away from it. If there is a threatening OB area left, tee up on that side, aim down the left side of the fairway, then try to fade your tee shot back into the fairway center. Conversely, if there is OB right tee up right and play for a draw.

Distance can be a great advantage in golf, but it can also be a disadvantage. Remember that your prime purpose on the tee shot is to place the ball in the best possible position for your second shot. Nearness to the hole would not be the best position, for example, if it would mean playing your second from a sharply sloping lie. Pick flat target areas.

Very rarely will a wild long driver consistently outdistance a shorter but straighter hitter. The shorter hitter's ball, landing in the fairway, will generally run far enough to catch up with the longer hitter's ball when it's checked by the rough as it frequently is if he's wild. Keep that in mind next time you play a big hitter.

Slope-consciousness is essential in assessing preferred driving areas and techniques. The first priority is to seek out the flattest possible area from which to play the second shot. Beyond that, fairway slopes can dictate which shape of tee shot you play. For example, if the ground in the landing zone runs sharply from right to left, a faded ball stands less chance of running into trouble. Conversely, a drawn ball will best fight a strong left-to-right slope.

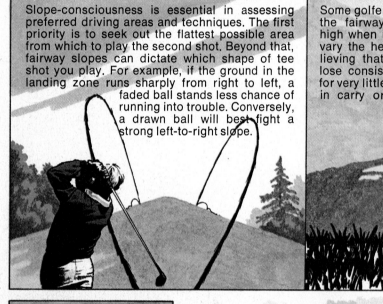

Some golfers tee the ball low when the fairway slopes downhill and high when it slopes uphill. I rarely vary the height I tee the ball, believing that by doing so I would lose consistency for very little gain in carry or roll.

Many high-handicappers equate the drive with a bunker shot—a horrible experience to be got out of the way as quickly as possible. I'd like to suggest that, for a change, you put *maximum concentration* into your tee shots. If you make the opening shot a good one the rest will become easier.

Never hurry that opening drive no matter how great the agony of having to perform "cold" in front of friends and waiting golfers. Nothing builds confidence better than a strong opening drive, and nothing saps it quicker than a poor one. So always concentrate your hardest on that first mood-setting shot of the day.

At the point of impact, these things must be happening to insure a successful drive: the club is traveling parallel to the ground; your mind is focused on generating maximum clubhead speed throughout the entire impact zone; your head is down and your eyes are on the ball; your hips are turning smoothly to allow greater leverage and clubhead speed; and your hands and wrists are releasing as the club swings through the ball.

IRON-SHOT STRATEGY

You may not be able to get my distance with your irons, but always consider the possibility of driving into the fairway with an iron, instead of into the trees with a wood, on a particularly troublesome hole. It's an elementary point, but one of many strategies often overlooked by club-level golfers.

For example, I can usually hit a 1-iron far enough from the tee to get home with my second shot at most par-4 holes. When I won the 1966 British Open at Muirfield, I nearly wore a hole in my 1-iron. I swung a wood from the tee only 17 times in 72 holes.

You'll often run into hardpan in summer. It causes the ball to fly lower and run farther than from softer turf. To overcome this I take one club longer (less-lofted) than normal, grip down on it, open the clubface, aim a little left of target, and play an intentional cut shot. The ball flies higher and settles softer off this type of shot. One other point: I do not try to sweep the ball off hardpan, but hit **DOWN** on it. There's less chance for error that way.

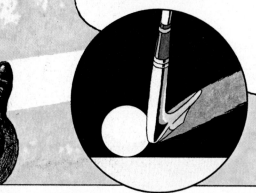

Always—and I mean **ALWAYS** —tee the ball on par-3 holes, or any other time you play your opening shot with an iron. A teed ball improves your percentages of making a solid, square impact. More than that, it reduces the risk of grass getting between the ball and the clubface, which, by diminishing backspin, will cause the ball to fly unpredictably.

Here's a tip on one of the toughest shots in golf—the pitch of between 50-80 yards, the three-quarter wedge or half 9-iron. You can choose to hit these shots hard or easy, but you should determine to hit them the same way every time. You'll never get the proper "feel" on these shots if you continually vary your swing power. I think most average golfers will get the best results from a firm-hitting style, because it lessens the tendency to quit on the shot.

Whichever way you go about these shots, be sure your backswing is long enough to prevent jabbing at the ball. "Feel" the correct length and power first with a few practice swings.

...ntentional high shots ...h irons should be part ...f every golfer's reper-...re. The technique is ...ple. Play the ball for-...rd off your left toe ...d open the clubface to ...e right slightly. Then ...ing normally.

You should know that the less loft an iron club has, the more control you have over the ball's **STARTING** direction. For example, it's much easier to hit the ball straight with a 2-iron for the first 50 yards than it is with a wedge. For this reason, when there is a question between two clubs, I tend to select the one with the **MINIMUM** amount of loft. This is particularly true into or across the wind, where I'll almost always make, say, a ¾-swing with a 9-iron rather than a full swing with a wedge.

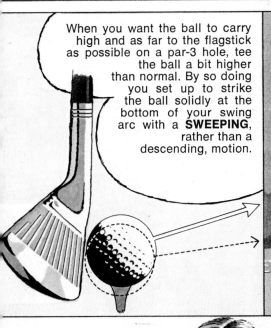

When you want the ball to carry high and as far to the flagstick as possible on a par-3 hole, tee the ball a bit higher than normal. By so doing you set up to strike the ball solidly at the bottom of your swing arc with a **SWEEPING**, rather than a descending, motion.

Always prac-tice hitting your iron shots **INTO** the wind. A tailwind will nose the ball down faster, and thus your shots will lose their true character. Also, avoid practicing with the wind blowing on your back. Fighting to hold the ball into a left-to-right wind can quickly lead to loss of left-side control.

Also, on the shorter irons, ...en there is little landing ...ea on the green, here's the ...y I play them to fly high ...d land softly. First, I sense ...at I'll need a slow and easy ...ing but one with firm control. ...ext I open the face of the club slightly ... the right—this is essential for maxi-...um height. During the swing, I grip ...mly with my left hand, but direct the ... with my right. It's a tricky shot to pull ...f, especially from a less-than-perfect ..., but it can be a great stroke-saver ...you learn to play it confidently.

119

LESSON 35:

PUTTING STRATEGY

Even if you have a super stroke, to putt well you must combine it with a positive mental attitude and good planning. Take enough time on **every** putt to study the line and the break and compute the ball's speed requirement. Figure out these factors until you can "see" the ball running to and dropping in the cup. Then be confident in your judgment—stick with your plan and do physically what you've decided mentally. Here are a few tips that have helped my mental approach to putting.

I don't switch putters very often. I recommend that you find a putter that gives you the best "feel," then stick with it. If you have trouble on the greens, the odds are 100-to-1 against the putter being at fault. More likely the problem rests with **you.** That's certainly true in my case.

Over-practicing can make you a worse, instead of better, putter! Your main concern on the course is "feel." That's what you want to develop on the practice green. When you've got a good feel going, quit practicing. Don't risk losing it by getting tired or losing your concentration.

My objective when I practice putting is to achieve a fluid, rhythmic feeling between my hands and the ball in a well-timed stroke. When I get the desired sensation on six or seven putts in a row, I stop.

Another thought on putting practice: if you're going to play a lot of different courses, don't practice too extensively on any one of them. You need to be able to judge speed on all the different surfaces you'll encounter. This is why I practice putting only at the course where I'm going to play—and then only enough to get my desired "feel."

Here's an example of how important I think mental attitude is in putting. I'd rather putt 10 feet straight downhill—even on a very fast green—than three feet across a side hill. I approach the 10-footer as a short putt, picking a target a few feet from the ball and then stroking as I would for a level putt of similar distance. Thus mentally I approach the 10-footer not as a 10-footer, but as a short putt. If I make the imaginary three-footer, I'll make the 10-footer!

On 40-footers and over, think distance rather than direction. Obviously you need to determine a **general** line for the putt, but, after you've done so, concentrate on distance — which means the speed of the ball relative to the green's texture and contour. If you're a regular three-putter, I guarantee this approach will help you tremendously.

If the courses you play most frequently have fast greens, you'd probably feel best with a light putter. The same applies if you have a tendency to putt the ball too hard. Conversely, on slow greens—or if you tend to stroke putts too lightly—a heavy putter might give you a better "feel."

The commonest, cheapest commodity on the golf course is advice. It's usually offered in a friendly spirit, but one place to completely ignore it is on the greens. Always do your own thinking on putts. No one else knows how hard you are going to hit the ball, so there's no way they can determine your line. Anyway, a lot of discussion about "break" diverts attention from distance, which in my view is the critical factor. Shut out the world as you prepare to putt, then do your own thing.

Yet another practice pointer: concentrate on the putts you'd normally expect to make, or have to make. By all means hit a few from 50 feet to gauge distance, but do your real work from 12 feet on in. You should expect to make any putt under 12 feet. If you learn to sink the three- and four-footers, you'll never need much long-distance practice.

Think you'd score lower if the cups were bigger? You can make them **look** bigger on the course by practicing putting to a tee stuck in the ground. I often do this, from 12 feet on down to four or five feet. It's surprising how much bigger this makes that 4¼-inch hole look.

Most very short putts are missed because the golfer quits—eases up on the stroke before or at impact. Here's one device that's helped me beat this dread disease. After determining the line, I aim for a spot just short of the hole over which the ball must travel. Then I consciously stroke the putt firmly, continuing to move the putterhead well through the ball toward my selected spot.

Here's another tip to try if you are really in bad trouble with the short ones: simply take the putter back **twice** as far as you had been doing, and stroke through a little easier. On a number of critical occasions in tournaments this gimmick has quickly smoothed out my stroke and re-established my control over the putterhead.

As I walk onto a green, I first check the direction the grass lies—the "grain." Next I examine the slopes between my ball and the cup, then the length of the grass. I also take wind into account if it is more than a mild breeze. All these factors relate to a putt's starting direction and speed. Consider them before you step up to the ball.

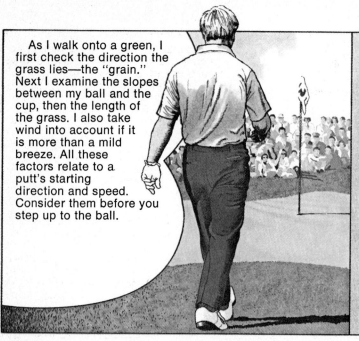

Standing perfectly erect is not the best angle for studying putts, because it does not give you a true picture of the ground's topography in your immediate vicinity. Nor is lying flat on your belly behind the ball necessarily the best angle. In fact, I think this worm's-eye view usually hides more than it reveals: you see only what's in the foreground. What you require is the position that gives you the best overall picture of the line. I find that squatting usually gives me the best possible vantage point.

On fast greens be particularly careful not to leave yourself those knee-knocking downhillers. Plan all your long approach putts so that you'll be putting uphill on the next shot.

Here's a system that might help you better assess double-breaking putts. Study both breaks in preparing to putt, but in stroking the ball, concentrate on the **first break only**. Plan to stroke the ball so that it will roll over the point where you've determined the second break will begin to take effect.

Leaving the ball short of the cup on short uphill putts is a cardinal golfing sin (of which I'm as guilty as the next man). This is the easiest of all putts to make. The back of the cup is higher than the front, which effectively increases the size of the target. So make a conscious effort on these putts to stroke firmly, and thus play the percentages one of the few times in golf they are in your favor.

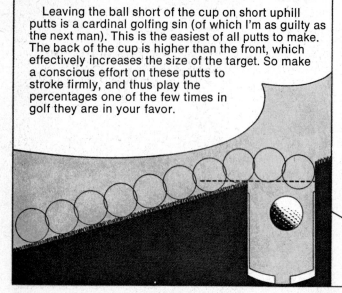

I'll nearly always putt rather than chip from just off the green if the ground is firm and free from wet or heavy grass. This "Texas wedge" shot is particularly useful when the lie is so thin as to make chipping risky. I use my normal putting stroke, hitting just a little more firmly than I would to cover the distance if it were entirely over the putting surface. One point I have to watch on these shots is head movement. It's a temptation any time you stroke a shot harder than normal to look where it's going too soon!

Most amateur golfers don't pay enough attention to grain. Look at the grass in all directions. When you can see a silvery sheen, you're looking down-grain. Remember that:

Grain against — decreases ball's speed (A).

Grain with—increases ball's speed (B).

Grain in direction of cross-slope—increases normal break (C).

Grain opposite cross-slope—decreases normal break (D).

Grain running toward hole—can hold ball straight on a downhill putt, even with a cross-slope that would cause ball to break several inches if it were going uphill (E).

Careful analysis of grain direction, especially on Bermuda-grass greens, will eliminate many missed putts that look "level" but actually break.

A

B

C   D   E

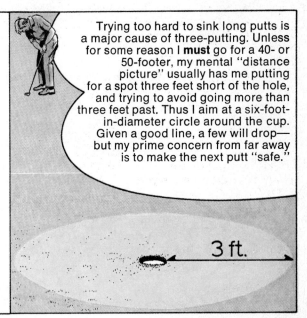

Trying too hard to sink long putts is a major cause of three-putting. Unless for some reason I **must** go for a 40- or 50-footer, my mental "distance picture" usually has me putting for a spot three feet short of the hole, and trying to avoid going more than three feet past. Thus I aim at a six-foot-in-diameter circle around the cup. Given a good line, a few will drop—but my prime concern from far away is to make the next putt "safe."

3 ft.

Have a good look around the area of the hole in sizing-up long putts, especially at times when grass growth is slow. Take into account a possible speed-up factor around the hole when greens are heavily worn. If foot traffic has been heavy, you could hit a 40-footer far past the hole if you base your stroke on the speed requirement of the first 20 feet.

So long as I'm not going steeply downhill, I favor a firm, bold stroke on short breaking putts, the "sliders" as we call them on tour.

To "die" this kind of putt into the hole with a gentle, delicate stroke requires that both your speed **and** direction be perfect. A firmer stroke eliminates the speed factor, allowing you to concentrate entirely on direction.

However, when you have a **downhill** "slider" on a fast green, "dying" the putt is probably the best approach. Allow for a little more break than normal, and try to stroke the ball so it will just topple into the front of the cup.

FIRM

DYING

I'll putt out of sand any time I think the percentages are in my favor—but they never are unless the trap is flat with no overhanging lip, the sand firm and I have an excellent lie. I use my normal stroke, but hit the ball on the toe rather than the center of the blade. I think this tends to cut down backspin and make the ball roll farther and more consistently.

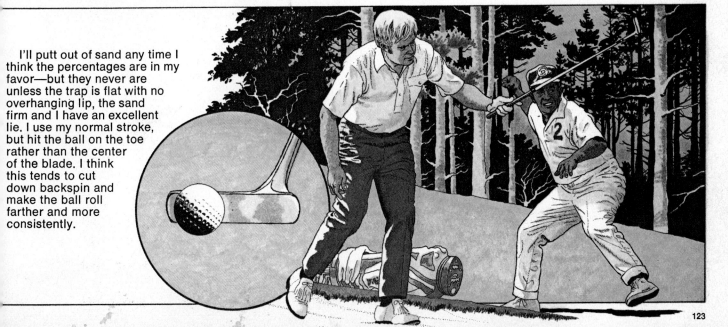

MATCH-PLAY STRATEGY

I agree with Bob Jones' philosophy that in match play a golfer should concentrate on his own game and on playing the course rather than his opponent.

Walter Hagen once said that he always assumed at the beginning of a round that he would probably make three or four mistakes. I think this attitude is one of the reasons he was such a great match player. Hagen could shrug off the frustration of a missed shot very fast, without disturbing his concentration and his overall positive perspective. A similar outlook would help most golfers.

On the greens, anytime your opponent's ball might serve as a backstop to prevent your putt running too far — as, for example, when his ball is directly behind the hole — let it lie. The rules allow your ball to strike it without penalty. But be wary when your opponent's ball is to the side of the hole. Your off-line putt might nudge his ball into the hole, which would save him one stroke.

In match play I never gamble when I don't have to. If I'm 1-up on the last hole and it's a par-5 with a creek fronting the green, I'll lay up so I can be sure of getting my third shot within two-putt range. This puts the pressure on my opponent to risk a big shot to make his birdie, and the odds are against him.

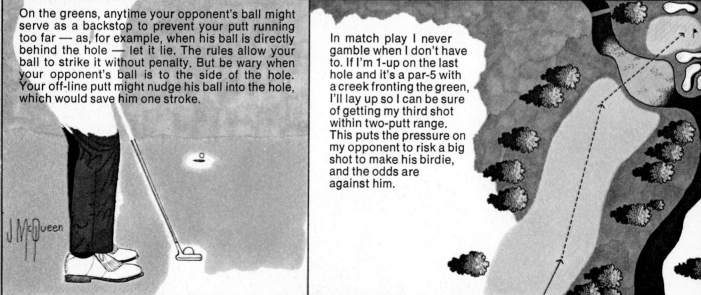

The worst strategy in match play is to assume that your opponent will make mistakes. This is a negative attitude that will quickly destroy your cool if your man turns out to be error-proof. It's better to assume he'll play well and resolve ahead of time that you'll have to do your best to win.

There is a difference, however, between respecting your opponent and being in awe of him. I like the old quotation, "A secret disbelief in the enemy's play is very useful." It's certainly better than an outright fearful approach, which often will communicate itself to an opponent and give him a psychological advantage.

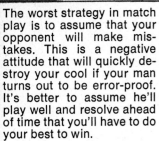

It's sometimes said that the measure of a match player is his performance coming down to the wire, but I believe you seriously jeopardize your chances by thinking you can always win with a late charge. I've won a lot of matches by building an early lead. You gain a considerable psychological advantage by drawing first blood, and the earlier and farther you can get ahead, the more pressure you place on your opponent.

Even though you are concentrating primarily on playing the course you can learn from your opponent. For example, if he hits first to a green, try to determine what club he is using and observe the flight of the ball and what happens to it when it lands. Be equally watchful around and on the putting green when he must chip or putt first over the same territory you'll have to negotiate.

Don't try to be a hero on the greens when you don't need to be. If your opponent is 20 feet from the cup in three and you're 40 feet away in two, concentrate on lagging your putt "dead" rather than trying to hole it. The percentages are that your opponent will miss. Even if he makes his putt you have lost nothing, whereas if he holed and you three-putted you've not only lost a hole but also suffered a nasty blow to your psyche.

When your opponent gets in serious trouble, play safely. Winning with a bogey is still winning. However, if I am behind in match play I often will take bigger risks with a recovery shot than I might in stroke play. This is simply because I have only one hole, rather than a bundle of strokes, to lose. And if I succeed, it could rattle my opponent.

Every so often you'll run into a fellow who you know is an inferior player, but who is beating the daylights out of you with his ability to get the ball up and down around the greens. My advice is to keep your cool and stick to your game plan. Unless the guy is a Deane Beman, the odds are that this is temporary. Not many golfers are able to live by their short games alone under pressure.

PART 8: ON PLAYING THE GAME

LESSON 37:
A WINTER REVIEW

Winter is a good time to review your game. Having infrequent opportunities to play isn't the handicap it might seem, because the reviewing process — properly done — is largely mental. What you're basically doing is making the diagnoses on which you'll later base your cures. First, sit down and be 100 per cent honest with yourself about two factors: (1) the game you played in the past year and (2) the game you're prepared to make the effort to play in the year ahead. Try not to kid yourself on either count, if you really would like to get more fun and satisfaction from golf.

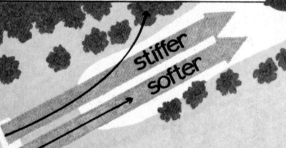

stiffer

softer

Let's suppose you discover you have been a weak driver, directionally or in terms of distance. The first thing to consider is the club you have been using. Of all their clubs, tournament golfers strive hardest to "custom fit" the driver to their individual swing styles. A little less weight or a little more loft could work wonders for thousands of handicap players. If direction is your problem, resolve to experiment at the first opportunity with a stiffer shaft. If distance has been a major limiting factor, try a "softer" shaft and more loft.

If experimenting in this manner is too much trouble, then resolve to play your *first five rounds* of the new year driving with whichever of your longer clubs feels most comfortable. This could be a 3-wood, or even a 4-iron. Whatever it is, use it for every drive—and amaze yourself with how much easier the game becomes when you keep the ball in play from the tee. Then work up to the driver, one club at a time, all the while trying to make the same swing you use with the favorite "easy" club.

NO.1
375 YD
PAR

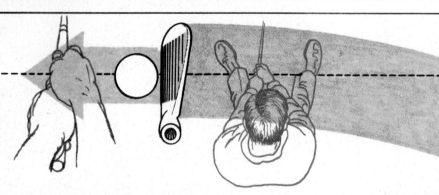

Should you choose the tougher alternative of improving your swing, then spend the winter imbedding in your consciousness the *basic objective* of the swing modifications you will make when you can get out onto the course. This is to deliver the clubhead to the ball traveling directly along the target line. Remember that the path of the club is determined largely by your setup alignment, and the angle of the clubface largely by the position of your hands on the club. A fine mental exercise is to work out for yourself, and then memorize, the club path/clubface alignment combinations that result in your best shots.

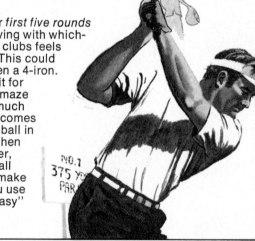

The shortest ro
to achieving
foregoing ba
objective is
course, lesso
from a compet
teaching prof
sional. That is w
I always tak
"fundamenta
course with Ja
Grout around
first of the ye
But here I'd sound a warning. Golf lesso
work only when you are willing to work. If y
doubt your ability to persevere with a forr
instruction program, you'd probably be bet
off simply going on trying to make the m
of what you've g

What were your biggest problems in the past season? What *specific* ones cost you most dearly? The way to answer those questions is to break the game into components and then evaluate your performance in each. I do this every winter. The components I use are: driving, approaching (hitting greens), recovery play (pitching, chipping and bunker play), putting, course management and self management. If you really think through your past year's performances, weakness in one or more of these areas likely will clearly show itself.

[f]or years in pro-ams I have watched [g]olfers who consistently slice and miss [g]reens to the right. They continually kid [t]hemselves that "*this* time it will go [s]traight," and thus always aim to hit [s]traight. If you habitually slice—and at [l]east 80 per cent of all golfers do—then [y]ou have two alternatives. Either you [c]an eliminate the fault by instruction [a]nd practice, or you can play with it by [d]eliberately aiming down the left side [a]nd letting the ball cut back on target. [If] you choose the latter—and by far [t]he easier—course, it may encour- [a]ge you to know that you're doing [e]xactly what Lee Trevino and I do [w]hen we play our bread-and- [b]utter fade, except you're [d]oing it on a larger scale.

The weakest area of my game has always been recovery play: pitching, chipping and—until the last couple of years—sand shots. It's also, I'd contend from my pro-am experience, the weakest part of most good amateur golfers' games. The reason usually is an imbalance in practice. The good golfer spends so much time keeping his long game in shape that he has insufficient time or energy for honing his short game. That's why I've built—and am now regularly using—a practice green and bunker in my backyard.

If your self-analysis reveals that you're a poor pitcher, consider the *firmness* with which you play the shots from 80 yards in. Overswinging, resulting in deceleration of the clubhead through impact, is a prime cause of poor wedge play. Swinging a short iron in the back yard or garage for a few minutes each day is an excellent way to stay in touch with the game through winter. If you mentally measure your length of backswing to a variety of imagined shot distances, you could do wonders for your pitching game. Be sure you swing *authoritatively* through the imaginary ball.

I once took some much-needed chipping lessons from Tom Weiskopf and Homero Blancas. What the fellows really reconfirmed for me is that the chipping stroke is nothing more complicated than a miniature golf swing. If your self-analysis reveals weakness in this area, some work on the living room rug simply trying to contact the ball solidly with a *natural, stress-free* swinging motion of the hands, wrists and arms could take a lot of strokes off your scores.

If putting turns out to have been your Achilles Heel, consider this fact of tour golf: misjudgment of speed (or distance) causes far more three-putts than misjudgment of line (or direction). And this further fact of tour golf: leaving the ball far short or far past the hole is a result of flawed stroking far more often than it is the result of faulty assessment of the force needed to propel the ball the required distance. Thus, if you have been weak on greens, look first to your stroke. Irrespective of putting mechanics, the objective is to repeatedly strike the ball solidly with the sweet spot of the putterface. Winter practice on a carpet is a sure way to develop that talent.

The ultimate test of a golfer's honesty comes when he gets around to analyzing his self and course management. For instance, how many shots would you have saved if you had never lost your temper, never got dispirited, always used your mind ahead of your muscles, always played within your known resources? If you answer those questions honestly and then really stick with the resulting resolutions, you cannot fail to play better in the coming year.

You can practice shotmaking and swing visualization any time, and the more you do the better you will play. Start by "seeing" a golfing situation that might typically confront you. Next, visualize the shot that would best deal with it, and actually "see" its flight in your mind's eye. Finally, imagine and mentally "feel" the swing you would need to execute the planned shot. I do this on every shot I play in tournament golf. You can do it in your living room or office for practice.

PRE-PLAY PREPARATION

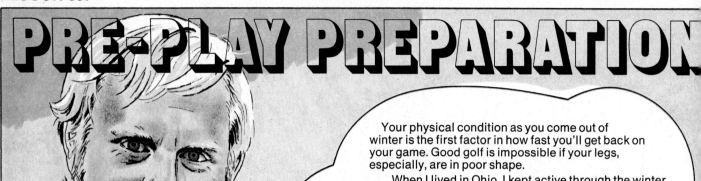

Your physical condition as you come out of winter is the first factor in how fast you'll get back on your game. Good golf is impossible if your legs, especially, are in poor shape.

When I lived in Ohio, I kept active through the winter playing basketball and handball. In Florida I play tennis and water-ski. Actually participating in a sport—paddle-tennis, skiing and squash are also great for the legs—is the best exercise, because it's competitive and fun. But any exercise is better than no exercise.

If that's too much for you, hit into a net in your garage, or whack plastic balls in your backyard once a week. The object is simply to prevent the 'feel' and timing of your swing from disappearing completely. If it does, you won't get back on your game until mid-summer.

Don't attempt to perfect a new method or work on specific swing mechanics under such difficult conditions. That's impossible.

Just hit a few balls often enough so that your muscles don't 'forget.' Once a week is plenty unless conditions are comfortable enough to encourage you to do more.

If it's absolutely impossible for you to hit any kind of ball, then at least go out and swing a heavy club for a few minutes two or three times a week. This isn't as beneficial as hitting balls, but it's better than nothing.

Now, when I can't get onto the course, I often use the artificial turf around my pool at home in Florida to putt on. (Deane Beman actually gave me a lesson on it that helped me win the 1971 PGA Championship.) For a really keen golfer a strip of this stuff might be a good investment . . . and maybe cut down the cost of rug renewals.

I practice putting indoors exactly the the way I do outdoors. I work first on the fundamentals of my grip, and my set-up to the ball and target. Then I work on the stroke, concentrating on smoothness and on striking the ball consistently on the putter's 'sweet spot.' (To locate this, bounce a ball on the putterface. When you feel no vibration, you've hit the sweet spot. Finally, I pick various targets and work on judging distance by trying to stop the ball on the selected mark.

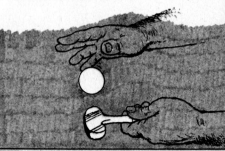

If you can't play a winter game, at least do some [jog]ging or strenuous walking as the golf season [app]roaches. Just cutting down on cab rides, or [usi]ng stairs instead of elevators, will help. Even [tho]ugh I'm now in pretty good shape all year [rou]nd, I still work out at home, stretching, [ben]ding and twisting before a new season. [No]thing too arduous. Just a few min-[ute]s a day to keep my muscles [in g]ood tone.

I recommend that even through the depths of winter, you somehow hit golf balls at least once a week. Where there's a will there's a way —in Columbus I'd clear snow for a place to swing, and then pick up the balls when it melted.

Golfers who don't touch a club in winter are usually so busy working on their long games once the courses open, they never have time to practice the short game. Thus it's Labor Day again before they start scoring well.

I strongly recommend using the living room rug to maintain your putting and chipping 'touch,' so that at least you don't have to learn these shots all over again when play resumes.

After a lay-off, I am usually eager to get out and play. Often I will deliberately increase this enthusiasm by showing myself golf films at home . . .

Just seeing golf in some form gives me an appetite to play and practice. It might do the same for you.

GO OUT AND HAVE FUN

When I lived in Ohio, the moment the course opened, I didn't go beat a thousand balls. Even if I'd wanted to, my legs wouldn't have been up to it. What I wanted to do was play, and I went out and *played*— often on frozen or soggy ground.

If the ground is very soft, you may unknowingly sink a little into it. This gives you the effect of a sidehill lie. Watch for this and adjust for it by choking down on your clubs.

Allow for the fact that your muscles are stiff and your action unpolished, but always do your best on every shot. In early season I don't get upset if I miss a shot, but on the course I try to make a good swing *every* time.

Don't worry about missing short putts your first few times out on poor greens. In fact, try to arrange with your group to give everything inside three feet. You're out for fun and exercise, not titles.

But I didn't play as though I was competing in the Masters. I'd try to hit a few balls before the round—enough so I could at least make contact on the course. If I couldn't hit warm-up shots, at least I'd do my three first-tee muscle-loosening exercises.

Eager as I was to play, I wouldn't make any midsummer bets. Until the course shaped up, I'd go out there primarily for exercise and fun—not for glory.

I'd always walk—as vigorously as possible to help re-condition my legs. When playing alone, I'd increase the walking—and the fun—by hitting two or three balls on each hole. Sometimes I'd forego putting to give myself time to walk 27 holes.

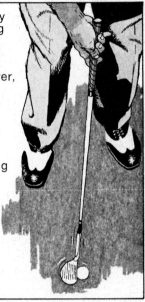

I'd concentrate particularly on my grip and setup to the ball, on swinging my hands high and making a full turn, and on starting down with my legs. I'd always try to play the proper club on every shot—hit tee shots with the driver, for example, not make things easy on myself by using a 3-wood or iron. But I would not make the game impossible by trying to play the ball as it lay.

Improving the lie when your swing is still rough at the edges and the ground is sodden or frozen is sheer common sense. Give yourself the best possible lie on every shot, then try to 'pick' the ball clean. Sweeping the clubhead through the ball is good swing training—apart from being the only way to hit effective shots from mud.

Early-season greens are usually bare and bumpy. Accommodate these irregularities in your stroke and your attitude to putting.

It is essential on long putts to get the ball rolling well. On poor greens I try to almost 'top' the ball—actually hitting its top half to maximize overspin.

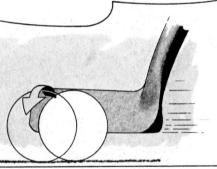

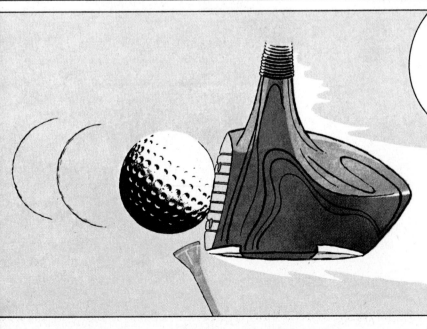

Don't get demoralized over the bad shots—you are bound to hit some in the rugged conditions of early season. Concentrate on regaining your tempo; on developing a good swing feel. But concentrate most on satisfying your pent-up desire to play. There'll be time later to work on specific aspects of your game.
Just keep trying to meet the ball solidly and squarely with the clubface.

LESSON 40:

START YOUR SERIOUS PROGRAM WITH A LESSON

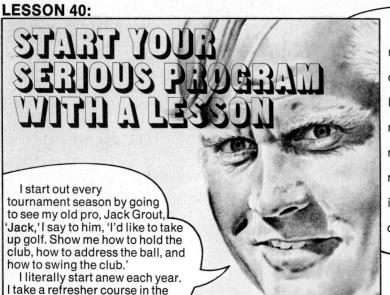

I start out every tournament season by going to see my old pro, Jack Grout, 'Jack,' I say to him, 'I'd like to take up golf. Show me how to hold the club, how to address the ball, and how to swing the club.'

I literally start anew each year. I take a refresher course in the basics, and I recommend that **you do so, too.**

Every golfer—including me—can unknowingly slip into bad habits. Frequently only a good teacher can spot such flaws. In my case, Jack Grout can get me back to fundamentals in minutes, whereas it might take me weeks of trial and error to iron out a basic fault on my own.

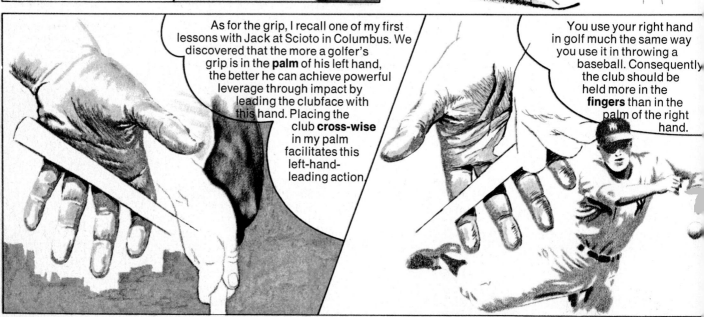

As for the grip, I recall one of my first lessons with Jack at Scioto in Columbus. We discovered that the more a golfer's grip is in the **palm** of his left hand, the better he can achieve powerful leverage through impact by leading the clubface with this hand. Placing the club **cross-wise** in my palm facilitates this left-hand-leading action.

You use your right hand in golf much the same way you use it in throwing a baseball. Consequently the club should be held more in the **fingers** than in the palm of the right hand.

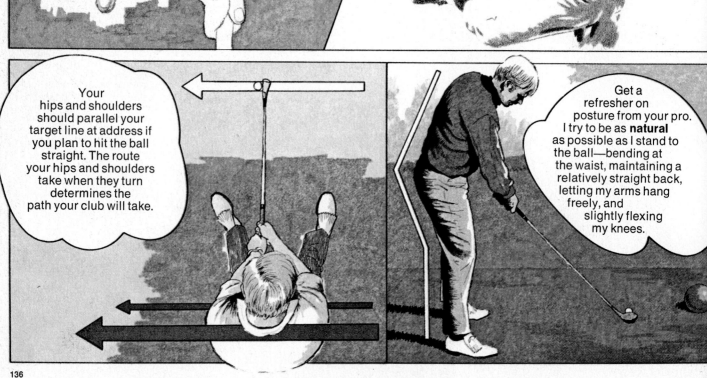

Your hips and shoulders should parallel your target line at address if you plan to hit the ball straight. The route your hips and shoulders take when they turn determines the path your club will take.

Get a refresher on posture from your pro. I try to be as **natural** as possible as I stand to the ball—bending at the waist, maintaining a relatively straight back, letting my arms hang freely, and slightly flexing my knees.

WHAT AND HOW TO PRACTICE

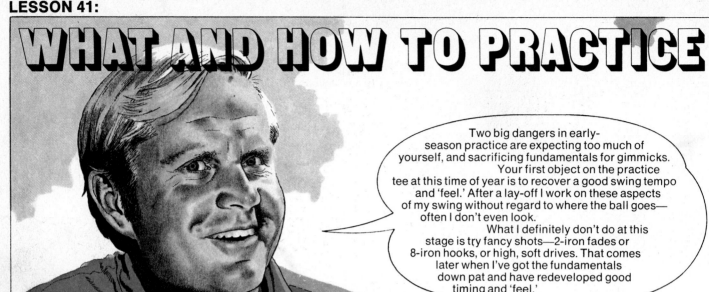

Two big dangers in early-season practice are expecting too much of yourself, and sacrificing fundamentals for gimmicks. Your first object on the practice tee at this time of year is to recover a good swing tempo and 'feel.' After a lay-off I work on these aspects of my swing without regard to where the ball goes—often I don't even look.

What I definitely don't do at this stage is try fancy shots—2-iron fades or 8-iron hooks, or high, soft drives. That comes later when I've got the fundamentals down pat and have redeveloped good timing and 'feel.'

How good a year you have largely depends on how hard you will practice the funda-mentals at the start of the season.

To me these are grip, aim and stance, head position, balance, a full body turn, high hands, the legs initiating the downswing, and smooth overall tempo. I concentrate and work on these areas one at a time as a prelude to bringing my game together.

Take a lesson—as I do—then stick to what you are told. Stay with it long enough to really give it a chance to work. If it simply won't work after a fair trial, go back and have another lesson.

At all cost, resist the urge to find a new swing or 'secret' every time you practice. That's simply a fast route back to your old faults.

J McQueen

Before you start ripping those drives, always loosen up and develop a sense of **feel** by hitting some shots with a short iron, then a mid-iron, and maybe even a long iron.

Golf is easier than many people believe. Many golfers' chief problem is simply that they won't persevere with fundamentals. They are like a friend I play with each year in the Crosby. We get him back to fundamentals and playing nicely to his handicap. But the moment he hits one bad shot on the course, he's off in search of a new theory. He's always in trouble.

Know **how** to practice, as well as what to practice.

If you've neglected the game all winter, taking a day off from work to blitz 1,000 balls is going to get you nothing but muscle strain and blisters. If you have a tendency to fire off balls like a machine gun, place your practice balls a couple of steps away from where you're hitting. That way you'll be **forced** to pause and think between shots.

Besides working toward a definite **goal** when you practice, always shoot to a definite **target**— a practice bag, yard marker, caddie. This not only builds correct alignment habits, but gives you a clear perspective of the distance you are hitting the ball relative to your target.

The practice tee is the place to train yourself to **picture** the ball in flight, and its positive result, before you actually swing. The ability to use imagination is one of the most valuable assets a golfer can possess.

After a lay-off, I never practice for more than an hour at a time. Any more than that and I start hitting the ball badly through sheer exhaustion.

A little practice at different times *often* is better than a lot of practice infrequently. When I'm rebuilding my game, I'll play nine holes, hit balls for half an hour, then play another nine.

10 NEW YEAR'S RESOLUTIONS

1. Decide at what level you want to play golf, then make a plan to achieve that goal. If you can't break 100, but think you'd be just happy as a 90-shooter, then just two or three lessons will probably do the job. If you're a 90-shooter who wants only to score in the 80s, improvement in your short game almost certainly offers the easiest route. If you seek to move from the 80s into the 70s, then your plan almost certainly must include considerably more practice than actual play on the course. If your target is par or better, then you must identify and correct even the most subtle flaws in your game, and engage in the maximum amount of meaningful competitive play.

4. If you are not as good a golfer as you would like to be, the reason almost certainly lies in either your grip or your setup to the ball, rather than in your swing motion. Resolve, therefore, once and for all to get these "statics" right. Do so before tampering with any other area of your game, preferably with the help of a qualified teacher.

5. Decide to acc the fact that, ir the final analy —the score golf is a game precision, not power. Long drives in them selves do not prizes. So res to try first and foremost to ke the ball in play the course— while, if you w learning to hit farther on the practice tee.

8. Read the Rules of Golf and resolve to play by them at all times. Few golfers who do not earn their living from the game know the Rules of Golf, and often inadvertently cheat. Sometimes they cheat themselves by not knowing the rules that work to their advantage.

7. If you regularly shoot more than 80, every time you think of an approach club make yourself take one more. I promise you that you will go over fewer greens this year than you were short of last year.

Promise yourself that you will never again hit a shot carelessly or half-heartedly or angrily. Apply this to practice as well as to actual play. I regard my lifelong habit of giving *every* shot I play my very best try—including on the practice tee or green—a big factor behind my ability to concentrate and compete hard.

3. Resolve not to quit, never to give up, no matter *what* the situation. Many of my major championship wins resulted largely from my simply hanging in as others faltered. A golf tournament or match is *never* over for you until your opponents have holed their last putt.

Determine to play within your own capabilities. You may be working your way out of the 80s into the 70s, but until you get there you will consistently fail in terms of scoring by pretending you are a better player than you are. Being realistic in assessing and playing shots—especially trouble shots—is good course management, not lack of courage.

Resolve to keep clearly in mind at all times the primary object of the golf swing, which is to deliver the clubface to the ball square to the target while traveling as fast as possible along the target line. Understand how all variations from that ideal cause the ball to move left or right, and apply this knowledge as your *starting point* in building your game.

10. Seek to understand the fundamentals of swing motion, built on a foundation of proper grip and setup, that achieve the objective stated in Resolution No. 9. Then resolve to abide by those fundamentals. They are few in number by comparison with the gimmicks that will tempt you, but they are the only "secrets" to good golf. We will review those fundamentals for you next month in closing this present series.

LESSON 43:
STARTING YOUNGSTERS

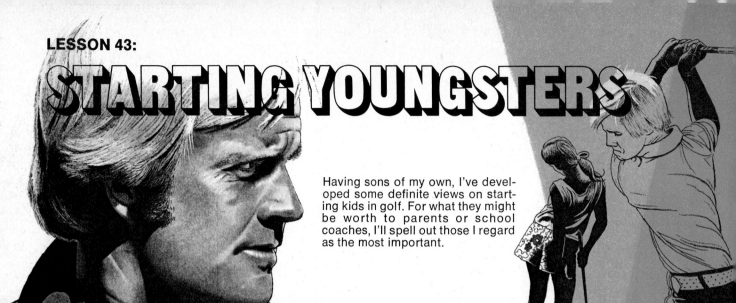

Having sons of my own, I've developed some definite views on starting kids in golf. For what they might be worth to parents or school coaches, I'll spell out those I regard as the most important.

Starting to Swing: Give the youngster a short iron and get him to swing it smoothly, to and fro, almost pendulum fashion, going no farther than three or four feet back or through. No ball . . . . just swinging with the hands and arms, making a natural wrist break going back and a natural roll on the through swing.

Backswing Development: First, build a big arc by encouraging the youngster to reach high—to reach for the sky. I don't care if the club comes so far around it hits him on the left leg, as long as he stretches his muscles fully. If he doesn't now, he won't later.

Second, encourage him to *swing* the club back with the help of its natural momentum, rather than "take" it back to a particular position.

Third, work with him on learning to swing the club straight back from the ball with a one-piece movement of hands, arms, hips and shoulders. As his strength increases, try to make him feel that he is delaying backswing wrist action until the weight of the club forces the wrists to cock.

Taking Lessons: There is no substitute for personal instruction and supervision by a competent teaching professional, especially at the beginning. The important thing is that the youngster isn't overloaded with technical advice, and that he understands exactly what he's asked to do — and why.

Staying on Target: Forget outside-in and inside-out swings for the time being. Simply encourage the youngster to try to make the clubhead travel out toward his target on every shot.

Gripping: A youngster with nothing to unlearn usually develops a correct grip more easily than an adult with a few swings under his belt. If the youngster lacks strength, though, his natural tendency will be to take a strong grip—hands well to the right. That's OK if it's all he can initially handle, but don't let him take it too far. The longer he uses it the tougher the habit will be to break.

As soon as the youngster develops sufficient strength, gradually move his hands into a more neutral position—more on top of the club. He'll push or slice the ball at first, but good swing habits and increasing strength will rectify that.

Grip style? I started with the inter-locking grip and have stayed with it, so I'm prejudiced in its favor. I think it knits the hands together better than the overlapping or baseball (10-finger) grip—especially a youngster's small hands.

Footwork: You'll teach a youngster good footwork fastest by getting him to practice swinging without lifting his heels. As the weight shifts the ankles roll freely inward—left going back, right coming down.

Balance: A fine way to teach a youngster to develop balance is to replace awareness of the ball with consciousness of making a good follow-through, then holding his finish position for a few seconds. If there's been much sideway tilt or head movement along the way, he won't be able to achieve this.

However, even a good lesson once a week, or whatever, is next to useless if a youngster doesn't practice between times. You have to be careful here, because if the youngster doesn't enjoy practice, too much accent on it may kill his enthusiasm for the game. This is especially true if his parents don't personally practice what they preach. The trick is to find ways to make practice fun.

If that doesn't work, at least encourage the youngster to play sports that will increase his strength, especially in his legs and back.

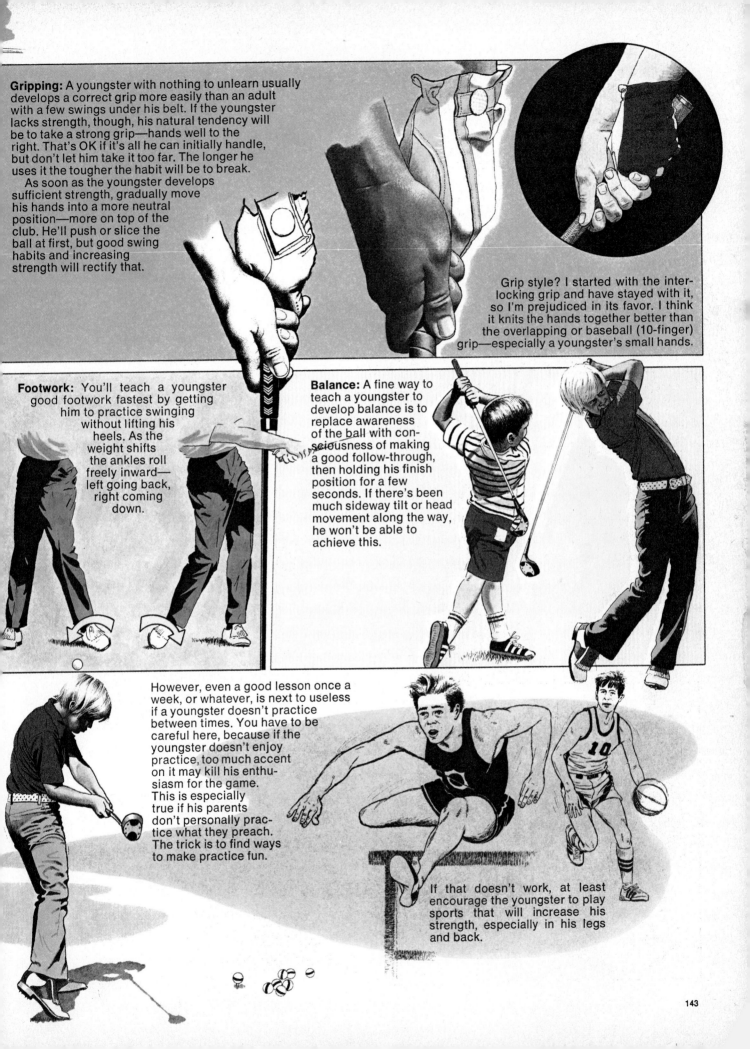

143

Clubs: I started at age 10 with a cut-down set of my father's clubs. But I was bigger and stronger than average and could switch to regular clubs within a year. Obviously, clubs must be tailored to size and strength, but I believe it's a wise policy to switch a youngster to adult clubs as soon as possible to forestall any possibility of him developing a short-club swing. He can always choke down on the regular clubs, and their added weight will help develop strength.

A youngster needs no more than three clubs to start. I'd recommend a 3-wood, 5-iron and putter. More clubs can be added as the player develops.

Observation: Children are great mimics. There is nothing better for their game than watching good golfers in action. Many will learn more about rhythm and swing tempo in one day at a pro tour or top amateur event than they would from a dozen lessons.

As they get older the lesson will extend, if they are really observant, to course management—an area of the game badly neglected in teaching youngsters.

Competition: Only when a youngster competes will he begin to understand fully the need for all he has been taught about golf. Suddenly all the effort and work will begin to make much more sense. Losing will be a useful experience for him, hopefully spurring him to greater effort. Winning will have the same effect in a happier way. It's what the game is all about, and you can't get into it too early.

LESSON 44:
WOMEN AND SENIORS

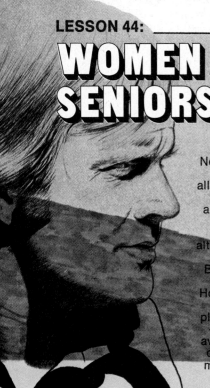

Never having taught golf, I'm not familiar with all the special problems of the senior player. Nor am I too knowledgeable about golf from the female standpoint—although golfing occasionally with my wife Barbara has given me a little insight there. However, my own golfing longevity—I've been playing 27 of my 37 years—increasingly brings awareness of the modifications that have to be made as strength and stamina decrease.

Distance is a problem for both seniors and women, and I think there are two reasons. The first lies in equipment. I've increasingly favored "light-swinging" clubs as I've got older, and I think I'll go more and more in that direction in the future. One reason is that clubhead velocity has twice the value of mass in terms of distance—the lighter the club the easier it is to swing through the ball fast. Also, the lighter the club, the less it takes out of you physically to swing it. This can be a big factor as one tires toward the end of a round. Softer shafts and lower-compression balls are other modifications that can benefit the physically weaker player, especially if he or she is more of a swinger than a hitter.

A second answer to sustaining distance lies in improving your precision in striking. I've always been impressed, when I've watched the top women professionals, with how squarely they hit the ball. It is the big factor behind their deftness at placing the ball near the pin with the fairway woods. It comes from muscular control and hand-eye coordination, not muscular effort. Improve your squareness of clubface delivery and, even though doing so may involve sacrificing a little clubhead speed, you will almost certainly improve your yardage average.

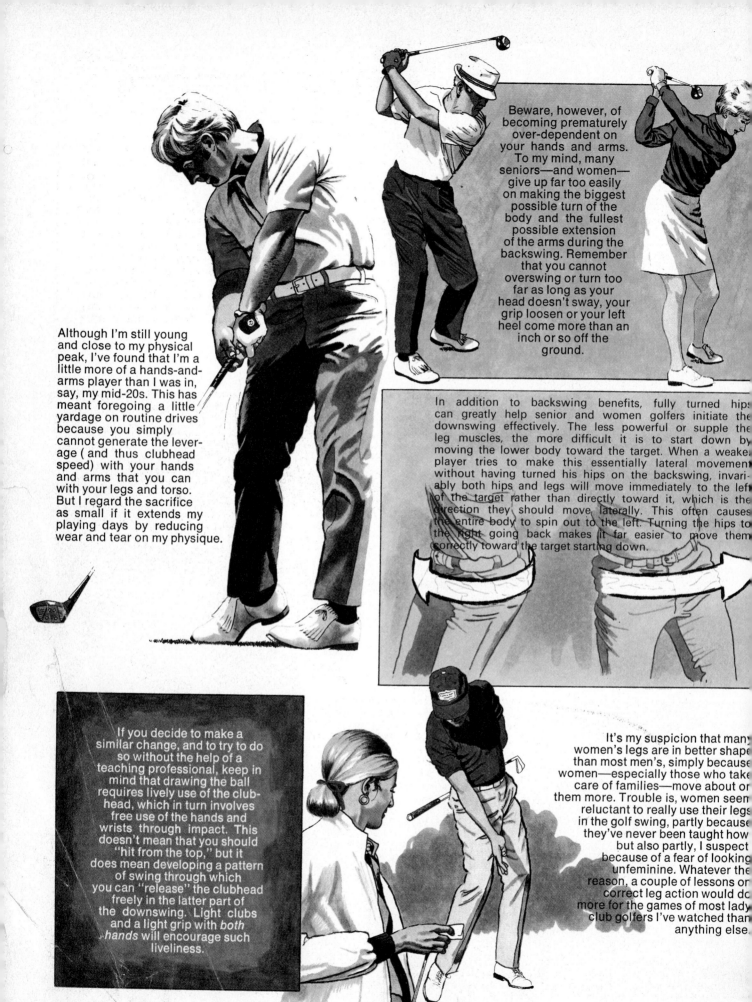

Although I'm still young and close to my physical peak, I've found that I'm a little more of a hands-and-arms player than I was in, say, my mid-20s. This has meant foregoing a little yardage on routine drives because you simply cannot generate the leverage (and thus clubhead speed) with your hands and arms that you can with your legs and torso. But I regard the sacrifice as small if it extends my playing days by reducing wear and tear on my physique.

Beware, however, of becoming prematurely over-dependent on your hands and arms. To my mind, many seniors—and women—give up far too easily on making the biggest possible turn of the body and the fullest possible extension of the arms during the backswing. Remember that you cannot overswing or turn too far as long as your head doesn't sway, your grip loosen or your left heel come more than an inch or so off the ground.

In addition to backswing benefits, fully turned hips can greatly help senior and women golfers initiate the downswing effectively. The less powerful or supple the leg muscles, the more difficult it is to start down by moving the lower body toward the target. When a weaker player tries to make this essentially lateral movement without having turned his hips on the backswing, invariably both hips and legs will move immediately to the left of the target rather than directly toward it, which is the direction they should move laterally. This often causes the entire body to spin out to the left. Turning the hips to the right going back makes it far easier to move them correctly toward the target starting down.

If you decide to make a similar change, and to try to do so without the help of a teaching professional, keep in mind that drawing the ball requires lively use of the clubhead, which in turn involves free use of the hands and wrists through impact. This doesn't mean that you should "hit from the top," but it does mean developing a pattern of swing through which you can "release" the clubhead freely in the latter part of the downswing. Light clubs and a light grip with *both hands* will encourage such liveliness.

It's my suspicion that many women's legs are in better shape than most men's, simply because women—especially those who take care of families—move about on them more. Trouble is, women seem reluctant to really use their legs in the golf swing, partly because they've never been taught how but also partly, I suspect because of a fear of looking unfeminine. Whatever the reason, a couple of lessons on correct leg action would do more for the games of most lady club golfers I've watched than anything else.

In striving to keep that big backswing turn going as long as possible, you'll probably have to permit a freer and fuller turn of your hips along with your shoulders. Don't fight that tendency. Remember, although Tom Weiskopf and other tour stars may hardly turn their hips today, Bobby Jones won 13 major championships turning his hips almost as fully as his shoulders. Too much hip turn is better than no hip turn for all but the strongest and most supple golfers. The main things to watch are that the hips follow, rather than lead, the shoulder turn and that your right knee always stays a little flexed.

A friend of mine who plays at a very tough course near my home in Florida actually cut his handicap in half—from 17 to 8—in his early 60s. He claims this was entirely a result of learning to draw the ball from right to left, rather than fading or slicing it from left to right. It took three months of three-times-a-week practice, no play on the course, and the help of a professional for him to do this, but now he's in seventh heaven, not only about his handicap but his much greater distance. My observation that almost all top senior amateurs and women professionals basically draw the ball would seem to support such an effort.

It may be stating the obvious, but I can't overstress physical fitness as a conditioner for good golf, especially for the less physically endowed player. In my experience the better shape you're in —especially your legs—the better you'll play, and this obviously has to become even more of a factor as the years advance. That's why, although I don't particularly enjoy it, I now exercise pretty energetically every morning and many evenings before retiring. And I expect to increase these regimens as I get older.

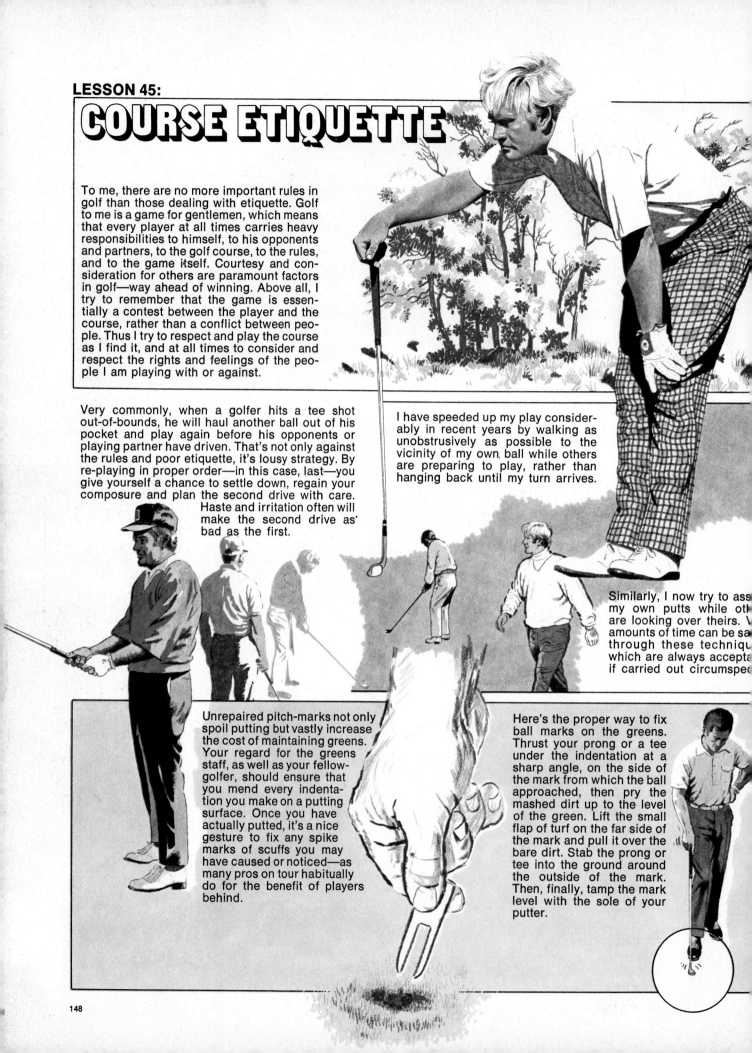

LESSON 45:
COURSE ETIQUETTE

To me, there are no more important rules in golf than those dealing with etiquette. Golf to me is a game for gentlemen, which means that every player at all times carries heavy responsibilities to himself, to his opponents and partners, to the golf course, to the rules, and to the game itself. Courtesy and consideration for others are paramount factors in golf—way ahead of winning. Above all, I try to remember that the game is essentially a contest between the player and the course, rather than a conflict between people. Thus I try to respect and play the course as I find it, and at all times to consider and respect the rights and feelings of the people I am playing with or against.

Very commonly, when a golfer hits a tee shot out-of-bounds, he will haul another ball out of his pocket and play again before his opponents or playing partner have driven. That's not only against the rules and poor etiquette, it's lousy strategy. By re-playing in proper order—in this case, last—you give yourself a chance to settle down, regain your composure and plan the second drive with care. Haste and irritation often will make the second drive as bad as the first.

I have speeded up my play considerably in recent years by walking as unobstrusively as possible to the vicinity of my own ball while others are preparing to play, rather than hanging back until my turn arrives.

Similarly, I now try to ass[...] my own putts while oth[...] are looking over theirs. [...] amounts of time can be sa[...] through these techniqu[...] which are always accepta[...] if carried out circumspec[...]

Unrepaired pitch-marks not only spoil putting but vastly increase the cost of maintaining greens. Your regard for the greens staff, as well as your fellow-golfer, should ensure that you mend every indentation you make on a putting surface. Once you have actually putted, it's a nice gesture to fix any spike marks of scuffs you may have caused or noticed—as many pros on tour habitually do for the benefit of players behind.

Here's the proper way to fix ball marks on the greens. Thrust your prong or a tee under the indentation at a sharp angle, on the side of the mark from which the ball approached, then pry the mashed dirt up to the level of the green. Lift the small flap of turf on the far side of the mark and pull it over the bare dirt. Stab the prong or tee into the ground around the outside of the mark. Then, finally, tamp the mark level with the sole of your putter.

Common courtesy demands that you give every player opportunity to do his best. Perhaps the best expression of this is the age-old tradition of standing quietly, out of vision and without any physical movement, while other golfers play their shots. Any violation of this tradition is at best bad manners and at worst gamesmanship.

Never hit the ball if there is even the slightest possibility that a player ahead of you hasn't moved out of range. Apart from the risk of causing serious injury, you cannot possibly give maximum concentration to a shot when you are the least bit conscious that the field of play isn't really clear. If there seems to be undue delay among the group ahead, try a "Fore!" rather than a missile in their midst.

One blatant cause of slow play—and an example of bad manners—is holding inquests and marking scorecards while loitering on or close to putting greens. Get moving as soon as you've putted out and do your ribbing and writing as you go.

I think the golfer who fails to clean up his mess in a sand trap should be banned from the game. There is no more frustrating sensation in sport than to walk into a bunker and find your ball impossibly situated in some careless or lazy fellow's foot or club print. The absence of a rake is no excuse for not smoothing the sand. You can take care of the marks easily with the back of a club.

It should hardly be necessary to remind any golfer to replace his divots, but I often have partners in pro-ams who seem oblivious to the craters they cut in the course. Probably they're relying on the caddie to do the job for them, but there's no harm in checking him out occasionally—or even doing the job yourself when the caddie forgets.

149

When you handle the flagstick, do so gently, being particularly careful not to let it damage the sides of the hole. If you find irregularities in the rim of the hole, take a few seconds —but only *after* you have putted—to tamp the earth back into shape for the following players.

Too many golfers spend far too much time searching for lost balls. As you start to look for a lost ball check the time on your watch. The rules allow you a five-minute search, and honesty demands that you do not exceed it.

A certain type of golfer seems to feel that letting others play through is something he shouldn't do. It's a dumb attitude, in that people breathing down your neck are bound to disturb your concentration —even if your obvious bad manners don't upset your psychic equilibrium. If you've lost a ball or are playing noticeably slower than the group behind, let them play through and get them off your back. And if a few holes later you find another group pressing you, give some serious thought to accelerating your pace of play.

Meeting one's obligations as a golfer is impossible without knowledge and understanding of the Rules of Golf. Every serious player gives time to acquiring that knowledge and understanding. Doing this not only prevents him from losing strokes and matches through ignorance, but it also enables him to capitalize on the advantages the Rules offer. In either instance, he can save himself the embarrassment of appearing to cheat through ignorance or he can be sure, if questioned by an opponent, that a decision he has made is indeed a correct one. In other words, he can be sure that his every act on the course is fairly done, which is strongly in keeping with the etiquette demanded by the game.

PART 9:
A REVIEW OF FUNDAMENTALS

BACK TO BASICS

This series has drawn from me just about everything I know about golf technique. Looking back, I find that there isn't one important element of the golf swing that hasn't been covered. What hasn't always been possible, however, is to present these elements in relationship to each other. Because the effective golf swing is essentially a continuous *flow of movement,* rather than a set of separate actions, I feel it is important that at least once in this series we look at the over-all swing, even though we must still describe the parts to make the whole.

This concluding lesson attempts to do just that. It serves as a review of what I regard as the fundamentals of the full golf swing, as well as a checklist for the coming season. I suggest that you use it as an overview, and as a regular reminder course, referring to preceding lessons when you need more detail on a particular technique.

THE GRIP

1 Your hands must work as a unit throughout the swing. Interlocking (my choice) or overlapping the little finger of the bottom hand around the first finger of the top hand encourages that. So does setting your hands parallel to each other on the clubshaft.

2 The alignment of your hands greatly affects the alignment of your clubface at impact. If your shots curve left, move both hands gradually counterclockwise or toward your target. If your shots curve right, move both hands gradually clockwise away from your target. You will have found your ideal grip alignment when most of your shots continue straight in their starting direction.

3 Although the hands function as a unit, the top hand must guide the club throughout the swing and stay firm as the lower hand applies power through impact. This demands that the top hand hold the club authoritatively. You can best achieve this by placing the club across the palm and then wedging it solidly against the butt of the hand with the last three fingers.

4 The lower wrist and hand must "release" freely through impact. You get this vital slinging-type action by gripping primarily with the fingers of the lower hand, which rids you of tension in the wrist and forearm.

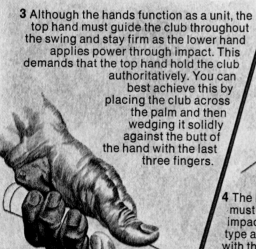

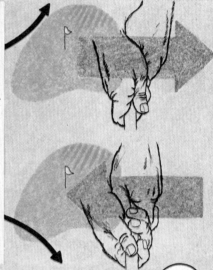

5 Consistency of grip configuration and pressure throughout the swing are critical to shot consistency. There are many ways to attain both. Mine is to firm up my hands just before I start the club back and then consciously try to maintain a feeling of unity and "firm passivity" in them from takeaway through the follow-through.

THE SET-UP

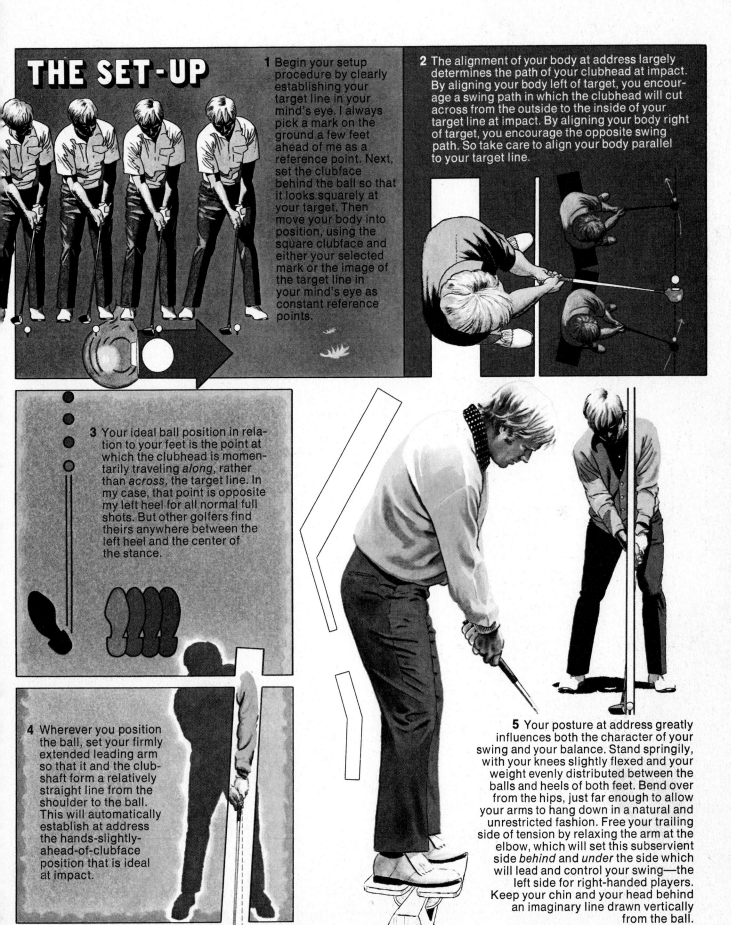

1 Begin your setup procedure by clearly establishing your target line in your mind's eye. I always pick a mark on the ground a few feet ahead of me as a reference point. Next, set the clubface behind the ball so that it looks squarely at your target. Then move your body into position, using the square clubface and either your selected mark or the image of the target line in your mind's eye as constant reference points.

2 The alignment of your body at address largely determines the path of your clubhead at impact. By aligning your body left of target, you encourage a swing path in which the clubhead will cut across from the outside to the inside of your target line at impact. By aligning your body right of target, you encourage the opposite swing path. So take care to align your body parallel to your target line.

3 Your ideal ball position in relation to your feet is the point at which the clubhead is momentarily traveling *along*, rather than *across*, the target line. In my case, that point is opposite my left heel for all normal full shots. But other golfers find theirs anywhere between the left heel and the center of the stance.

4 Wherever you position the ball, set your firmly extended leading arm so that it and the club-shaft form a relatively straight line from the shoulder to the ball. This will automatically establish at address the hands-slightly-ahead-of-clubface position that is ideal at impact.

5 Your posture at address greatly influences both the character of your swing and your balance. Stand springily, with your knees slightly flexed and your weight evenly distributed between the balls and heels of both feet. Bend over from the hips, just far enough to allow your arms to hang down in a natural and unrestricted fashion. Free your trailing side of tension by relaxing the arm at the elbow, which will set this subservient side *behind* and *under* the side which will lead and control your swing—the left side for right-handed players. Keep your chin and your head behind an imaginary line drawn vertically from the ball.

STARTING BACK

1 If you start your swing from a static or rigid position, it is certain to be jerky, uncoordinated and forced. So stay gently in motion as you finalize your setup, preferably with a waggle or two, or a slight to-and-froing of your weight. Then start the clubhead back as a reflex to a triggering movement.

2 My takeaway "trigger" is a conscious firming of my grip combined with a slight swiveling of my head to my right to facilitate the fullest possible coiling of my shoulders going back. Other top golfers favor a forward press of the hands and arms, or a targetward shift of the knees, to get started. Identify your own most effective trigger, then make it a habit.

3 Once triggered into action, my primary objective starting back is coordinated motion of my left side—perfect synchronization of the one-piece extension of my left hand, arm and club with the turning of the left side of my torso. Because this start programs the remainder of the swing, I am certain to mis-hit any shot that I do not begin in "one piece" with my left side fully in control.

4 For me the finest way way to ensure a one-piece, left-sided takeaway is to start the club away from the ball extremely slowly. Indeed, it is my conviction that you cannot start a golf club back too slowly so long as you *swing* it away from the the ball. Obviously the momentum of the club quickly increases after the first couple of feet. But covering the first two or three feet as *deliberately* as possible is the best way I know to prevent any one part of the body from jumping ahead of any other part.

5 Fashions come and go in start-back techniques, but here is the technique that has served me well for 20 years: (1) I try to swing the club straight back from the ball, without breaking my wrists, for as long as the turning of my shoulders and hips and extension of my arms will allow, so that I may achieve the widest possible swing arc. (2) I try to keep the clubface as square to the target line as possible for as long as possible without rotating my hands and arms. (3) I try to keep my left arm and the club in a straight line until the sheer momentum of the swinging clubhead causes my wrists to cock naturally.

TO THE TOP

1 Distance comes from clubhead speed squarely applied, clubhead speed comes from leverage, leverage comes from torsion, and torsion comes from backswing arm extension and body coiling. That's why I—and most modern tour golfers—emphasize the legs and body rather than the hands and arms.

2 Maximum backswing extension comes from the fullest and highest possible arm swing. To achieve it, your left arm and the club must remain in a straight line until the weight of the swinging clubhead naturally causes that hinging of your wrists as your arms begin to "reach for the sky."

3 Maximum backswing coiling comes from the fullest possible body turn. Your shoulders must continue to turn throughout the backswing in concert with your extended arms. To facilitate that, your hips also must turn—but only in response to your shoulder turn and always as *followers* of the shoulders, not *leaders*.

4 To create maximum torsion through maximum extension and coiling, and also to sustain the plane and arc of swing you have established at address, you must swing around a fixed axis. Your upper "anchor" is the back of your neck—do not let it move in any direction at any point in the backswing. Your lower "anchor" is your right knee (left for southpaws)—keep it flexed, with the weight on the inside of the foot throughout the backswing.

5 If you have extended and coiled fully going back, you will not be able to retain your top-of-swing position for more than an instant. The torsion between the lower and upper halves of your body will be so great that your muscles will demand immediate release. Anything short of that kind of reflexive start to the through-swing indicates lack of arm-club extension, or shoulder-hip coiling, or both.

DOWN AND THROUGH

1 The most common fault in golf is "hitting from the top"—throwing the clubhead at the ball with the hands and shoulders from the top of the backswing. Its common cause is lack of backswing torsion. If you simply lift the club up with your hands and arms, you have no alternative but to throw it down with them. Wind your body up like a spring going back and you will begin to unwind correctly —with your legs—entirely reflexively, without having to think about it.

2 Every good golfer's downswing begins before he completes his backswing. His knees are moving laterally — targetward — while his arms are still extending and his shoulders still turning backward. The ideal way to achieve this all-important targetward leg movement is reflexively — as an automatic response to backswing torsion. But, if you need a conscious thought, make it: "Wait for the legs to work before the hands start down."

3 Almost simultaneously with his lateral leg movement, the good golfer's hips begin to unwind *toward* the target to make room for his arms to swing freely past his body. Again, this is ideally a reflexive action, the natural reaction to backswing body torsion. But if you have to do it consciously, make your thought: "Keep the shoulders back while the hips uncoil."

4 Once your legs and hips have started you down, make no attempt to hold back your arms and hands. On full shots, I want my arms and hands to swing the club through the ball as fast and freely as they possibly can, providing only that they *follow* my lower-body actions. To me, "hitting from the top" is cured by accelerating leg-and-hip action, not by inhibiting arm-and-hand action.

5 One absolute through-swing principle, whatever your level of golf or type of swing— keep your head *behind* the the ball until well after impact, even though the momentum of the club may force you to let it swivel targetward. Swaying the head and upper body forward during the downswing is the second most common fault in golf —and maybe *the* most destructive.

TIMING

1 Those, then, are the fundamental mechanics and motions of the golf swing as I see them. To close, I want to remind you that the key to using them best is timing. And what is timing? To me it's the result of tempo and rhythm, tempo being the over-all *pace* of the swing, and rhythm being the variations of pace within the over-all swing tempo.

2 Your swing tempo will depend largely on your personality. High-strung people naturally swing fast, while most deliberate types swing comparatively slowly. And I recommend you stay with what's natural because, under pressure, you definitely will revert to it. The trick is to seek *smoothness* within your own natural tempo.

3 One way to attain smoothness is to swing on a big scale, which means motivating the club more with the body than the hands and arms. Think for a moment about all the movements you make in everyday living and it becomes obvious that, the bigger the muscle groups, the more deliberately and thus the more smoothly they function. That's one reason I'm glad I learned legs-and-body golf as a kid.

4 There are two crisis points that can affect tempo and rhythm. One is the takeaway and the other the transition from backswing to through-swing. The way you start the club back sets the tempo for everything that comes later, which is why I strive so hard to make that action *deliberate.* But, having established a good "tempo," you still have to maintain its rhythm in the danger area where the swing changes direction. One sensation that helps me to do so is that of consciously feeling the weight of the clubhead against the tension of the shaft for as long as possible into the downswing.

5 Finally, let me give you the one thought that more than any other has helped my timing over 25 years of golf: "Swing the hands and arms at the same pace coming down as going up." Obviously, this doesn't actually happen—the hands and arms are going to travel a heck of a lot faster coming down than going up. But that doesn't matter. What does is that the *thought* of identical pace up and down produces my ideal tempo, my smoothest rhythm and therefore my best timing.